The Perfect Wagnerite: A Commentary On The Niblung's Ring

The Perfect Wagnerite: A Commentary on

Table of Contents

The Perfect Wagnerite: A Commentary on

Bernard Shaw

Kessinger Publishing reprints thousands of hard–to–find books!

Visit us at http://www.kessinger.net

Preface to the First German Edition

In reading through this German version of my book in the Manuscript of my friend Siegfried Trebitsch, I was struck by the inadequacy of the merely negative explanation given by me of the irrelevance of Night Falls On The Gods to the general philosophic

1

scheme of The Ring. That explanation is correct as far as it goes; but, put as I put it, it now seems to me to suggest that the operatic character of Night Falls On The Gods was the result of indifference or forgetfulness produced by the lapse of twenty–five years between the first projection of the work and its completion. Now it is clear that in whatever other ways Wagner may have changed, he never became careless and he never became indifferent. I have therefore inserted a new section in which I show how the revolutionary history of Western Europe from the Liberal explosion of 1848 to the confused attempt at a socialist, military, and municipal administration in Paris in 1871 (that is to say, from the beginning of The Niblung's Ring by Wagner to the long–delayed completion of Night Falls On The Gods), demonstrated practically that the passing away of the present order was going to be a much more complicated business than it appears in Wagner's Siegfried. I have therefore interpolated a new chapter which will perhaps induce some readers of the original English text to read the book again in German.

For some time to come, indeed, I shall have to refer English readers to this German edition as the most complete in existence.

My obligation to Herr Trebitsch for making me a living German author instead of merely a translated English one is so great that I am bound to point out that he is not responsible for my views or Wagner's, and that it is as an artist and a man of letters, and not as a propagandist, that he is conveying to the German speaking peoples political criticisms which occasionally reflect on contemporary authorities with a European reputation for sensitiveness. And as the very sympathy which makes his translations so excellent may be regarded with suspicion, let me hasten to declare I am bound to Germany by the ties that hold my nature most strongly. Not that I like the average German: nobody does, even in his own country. But then the average man is not popular anywhere; and as no German considers himself an average one, each reader will, as an exceptional man, sympathize with my dislike of the common herd. And if I cannot love the typical modern German, I can at least pity and understand him. His worst fault is that he cannot see that it is possible to have too much of a good thing. Being convinced that duty, industry, education, loyalty, patriotism and respectability are good things (and I am magnanimous enough to admit that they are not altogether bad things when taken in strict moderation at the right time and in the right place), he indulges in them on all occasions shamelessly and excessively. He commits hideous crimes when crime is presented to him as part of his duty; his craze for work is more ruinous than the craze for drink; when he can afford secondary education for his sons you find three out of every five of them with their minds lamed for life by examinations which only a thoroughly wooden head could go through with impunity; and if a king is patriotic and respectable (few kings are) he puts up statues to him and exalts him above Charlemagne and Henry the Fowler. And when he meets a man of genius, he instinctively insults him, starves him, and, if possible, imprisons and kills him.

Now I do not pretend to be perfect myself. Heaven knows I have to struggle hard enough every day with what the Germans call my higher impulses. I know too well the temptation to be moral, to be self–sacrificing, to be loyal and patriotic, to be respectable and well–spoken of. But I wrestle with it and—as far as human fraility will allow—conquer it, whereas the German abandons himself to it without scruple or reflection, and is actually proud of his pious intemperance and self–indulgence. Nothing will cure him of this mania. It may end in starvation, crushing taxation, suppression of all freedom to try new social experiments and reform obsolete institutions, in snobbery, jobbery, idolatry, and an omnipresent tyranny in which his doctor and his schoolmaster, his lawyer and his priest, coerce him worse than any official or drill sergeant: no matter: it is respectable, says the German, therefore it must be good, and cannot be carried too far; and everybody who rebels against it must be a rascal. Even the Social–Democrats in Germany differ from the rest only in carrying academic orthodoxy beyond human endurance—beyond even German endurance. I am a Socialist and a Democrat myself, the hero of a hundred platforms, one of the leaders of the most notable Socialist organizations in England. I am as conspicuous in English Socialism as Bebel is in German Socialism; but do you suppose that the German Social–Democrats tolerate me? Not a bit of it. I have begged again and again to be taken to the bosom of my German comrades. I have pleaded that the Super–Proletarians of all lands should unite. I have pointed out that the German Social–Democratic party has done nothing at its Congresses for the last ten years except the things I told them to do ten years before, and that its path is white with the bones of the Socialist superstitions I and my fellow Fabians have slain. Useless. They do not care a rap whether I am a Socialist or not. All they want to know is; Am I orthodox? Am I correct in my revolutionary views? Am I reverent to the revolutionary authorities? Because I am a genuine free–thinker they look at me as a policeman looks at a midnight prowler or as a Berlin bourgeois looks at a suspicious foreigner. They ask "Do you believe that Marx was omniscient and infallible; that Engels was his prophet; that Bebel and Singer are his inspired apostles; and that Das Kapital is the Bible?" Hastening in my innocence to clear myself of what I regard as an accusation of credulity and ignorance, I assure them earnestly that I know ten times as much of economics and a hundred times as much of practical administration as Marx did; that I knew Engels personally and rather liked him as a witty and amiable old 1848 veteran who despised modern Socialism; that I regard Bebel and Singer as men of like passions with myself, but considerably less advanced; and that I read Das Kapital in the year 1882 or thereabouts, and still consider it one of the most important books of the nineteenth century because of its power of changing the minds of those who read it, in spite of its unsound capitalist economics, its parade of quotations from books which the author had either not read or not understood, its affectation of algebraic formulas, and its general attempt to disguise a masterpiece of propagandist journalism and prophetic invective as a drily scientific treatise of the sort that used to impose on people in 1860, when any book that pretended to be scientific was accepted as a Bible. In those days Darwin and Helmholtz were the real fathers of the Church; and nobody would listen to religion, poetry or rhetoric; so that even Socialism had to call itself "scientific," and predict the date of the revolution, as if it were a comet, by calculations founded on "historic laws."

To my amazement these reasonable remarks were received as hideous blasphemies; none of the party papers were allowed to print any word of mine; the very Revisionists themselves found that the scandal of my heresy damaged them more than my support aided them; and I found myself an outcast from German Social-Democracy at the moment when, thanks to Trebitsch, the German bourgeoisie and nobility began to smile on me, seduced by the pleasure of playing with fire, and perhaps by Agnes Sorma's acting as Candida.

Thus you may see that when a German, by becoming a Social-Democrat, throws off all the bonds of convention, and stands free from all allegiance to established religion, law, order, patriotism, and learning, he promptly uses his freedom to put on a headier set of chains; expels anti-militarists with the blood-thirstiest martial anti-foreign ardor; and gives the Kaiser reason to thank heaven that he was born in the comparative freedom and Laodicean tolerance of Kingship, and not in the Calvinistic bigotry and pedantry of Marxism.

Why, then, you may ask, do I say that I am bound to Germany by the ties that hold my nature most strongly? Very simply because I should have perished of despair in my youth but for the world created for me by that great German dynasty which began with Bach and will perhaps not end with Richard Strauss. Do not suppose for a moment that I learnt my art from English men of letters. True, they showed me how to handle English words;

but if I had known no more than that, my works would never have crossed the Channel. My masters were the masters of a universal language: they were, to go from summit to summit, Bach, Handel, Haydn, Mozart, Beethoven and Wagner. Had the Germans understood any of these men, they would have hanged them. Fortunately they did not understand them, and therefore only neglected them until they were dead, after which they learnt to dance to their tunes with an easy conscience. For their sakes Germany stands consecrated as the Holy Land of the capitalist age, just as Italy, for its painters' sakes, is the Holy Land of the early unvulgarized Renascence; France, for its builders' sakes, of the age of Christian chivalry and faith; and Greece, for its sculptors' sakes, of the Periclean age.

These Holy Lands are my fatherlands: in them alone am I truly at home: all my work is but to bring the whole world under this sanctification.

And so, O worthy, respectable, dutiful, patriotic, brave, industrious German reader, you who used to fear only God and your own conscience, and now fear nothing at all, here is my book for you; and—in all sincerity—much good may it do you!

London, 23rd. October 1907.

PREFACE TO THE SECOND EDITION

The preparation of a Second Edition of this booklet is quite the most unexpected literary task that has ever been set me. When it first appeared I was ungrateful enough to remonstrate with its publisher for printing, as I thought, more copies than the most sanguine Wagnerite could ever hope to sell. But the result proved that exactly one person buys a copy on every day in the year, including Sundays; and so, in the process of the suns, a reprint has become necessary.

Save a few verbal slips of no importance, I have found nothing to alter in this edition. As usual, the only protests the book has elicited are protests, not against the opinions it expresses, but against the facts it records. There are people who cannot bear to be told that their hero was associated with a famous Anarchist in a rebellion; that he was proclaimed as "wanted" by the police; that he wrote revolutionary pamphlets; and that his picture of Niblunghome under the reign of Alberic is a poetic vision of unregulated industrial capitalism as it was made known in Germany in the middle of the nineteenth century by Engels's Condition of the Laboring classes in England. They frantically deny these facts, and then declare that I have connected them with Wagner in a paroxysm of senseless perversity. I am sorry I have hurt them; and I appeal to charitable publishers to bring out a new life of Wagner, which shall describe him as a court musician of unquestioned fashion and orthodoxy, and a pillar of the most exclusive Dresden circles. Such a work, would, I believe, have a large sale, and be read with satisfaction and reassurance by many lovers of Wagner's music.

As to my much demurred−to relegation of Night Falls On The Gods to the category of grand opera, I have nothing to add or withdraw. Such a classification is to me as much a matter of fact as the Dresden rising or the police proclamation; but I shall not pretend that it is a matter of such fact as everybody's judgment can grapple with. People who prefer grand opera to serious music−drama naturally resent my placing a very grand opera below a very serious music−drama. The ordinary lover of Shakespeare would equally demur to my placing his popular catchpenny plays, of which As You Like It is an avowed type, below true Shakespearean plays like Measure for Measure. I cannot help that. Popular dramas and operas may have overwhelming merits as enchanting make−believes; but a poet's sincerest vision of the world must always take precedence of his prettiest fool's paradise.

As many English Wagnerites seem to be still under the impression that Wagner composed Rienzi in his youth, Tannhauser and Lohengrin in his middle age, and The Ring in his later years, may I again remind them that The Ring was the result of a political convulsion which occurred when Wagner was only thirty−six, and that the poem was completed when he was forty, with thirty more years of work before him? It is as much a first essay in political philosophy as Die Feen is a first essay in romantic opera. The attempt to recover its spirit twenty years later, when the music of Night Falls On The Gods was added, was an attempt to revive the barricades of Dresden in the Temple of the Grail. Only those who have never had any political enthusiasms to survive can believe that such an attempt could succeed. G. B. S.

London, 1901

Preface to the First Edition

This book is a commentary on The Ring of the Niblungs, Wagner's chief work. I offer it to those enthusiastic admirers of Wagner who are unable to follow his ideas, and do not in the least understand the dilemma of Wotan, though they are filled with indignation at the irreverence of the Philistines who frankly avow that they find the remarks of the god too often tedious and nonsensical. Now to be devoted to Wagner merely as a dog is devoted to his master, sharing a few elementary ideas, appetites and emotions with him, and, for the rest, reverencing his superiority without understanding it, is no true Wagnerism. Yet nothing better is possible without a stock of ideas common to master and disciple. Unfortunately, the ideas of the revolutionary Wagner of 1848 are taught neither by the education nor the experience of English and American gentlemen–amateurs, who are almost always political mugwumps, and hardly ever associate with revolutionists. The earlier attempts to translate his numerous pamphlets and essays into English, resulted in ludicrous mixtures of pure nonsense with the absurdest distorsions of his ideas into the ideas of the translators. We now have a translation which is a masterpiece of interpretation and an eminent addition to our literature; but that is not because its author, Mr. Ashton Ellis, knows the German dictionary better than his predecessors. He is simply in possession of Wagner's ideas, which were to them inconceivable.

All I pretend to do in this book is to impart the ideas which are most likely to be lacking in the conventional Englishman's equipment. I came by them myself much as Wagner did, having learnt more about music than about anything else in my youth, and sown my political wild oats subsequently in the revolutionary school. This combination is not common in England; and as I seem, so far, to be the only publicly articulate result of it, I venture to add my commentary to what has already been written by musicians who are no revolutionists, and revolutionists who are no musicians. G. B. S.

PRELIMINARY ENCOURAGEMENTS

A few of these will be welcome to the ordinary citizen visiting the theatre to satisfy his curiosity, or his desire to be in the fashion, by witnessing a representation of Richard Wagner's famous Ring of the Niblungs.

First, The Ring, with all its gods and giants and dwarfs, its water−maidens and Valkyries, its wishing−cap, magic ring, enchanted sword, and miraculous treasure, is a drama of today, and not of a remote and fabulous antiquity. It could not have been written before the second half of the nineteenth century, because it deals with events which were only then consummating themselves. Unless the spectator recognizes in it an image of the life he is himself fighting his way through, it must needs appear to him a monstrous development of the Christmas pantomimes, spun out here and there into intolerable lengths of dull conversation by the principal baritone. Fortunately, even from this point of view, The Ring is full of extraordinarily attractive episodes, both orchestral and dramatic. The nature music alone—music of river and rainbow, fire and forest—is enough to bribe people with any love of the country in them to endure the passages of political philosophy in the sure hope of a prettier page to come. Everybody, too, can enjoy the love music, the hammer and anvil music, the clumping of the giants, the tune of the young woodsman's horn, the trilling of the bird, the dragon music and nightmare music and thunder and lightning music, the profusion of simple melody, the sensuous charm of the orchestration: in short, the vast extent of common ground between The Ring and the ordinary music we use for play and pleasure. Hence it is that the four separate music−plays of which it is built have become popular throughout Europe as operas. We shall presently see that one of them, Night Falls On The Gods, actually is an opera.

It is generally understood, however, that there is an inner ring of superior persons to whom the whole work has a most urgent and searching philosophic and social significance. I profess to be such a superior person; and I write this pamphlet for the assistance of those who wish to be introduced to the work on equal terms with that inner circle of adepts.

My second encouragement is addressed to modest citizens who may suppose themselves to be disqualified from enjoying The Ring by their technical ignorance of music. They may dismiss all such misgivings speedily and confidently. If the sound of music has any power to move them, they will find that Wagner exacts nothing further. There is not a single bar of "classical music" in The Ring—not a note in it that has any other point than the single direct point of giving musical expression to the drama. In classical music there are, as the analytical programs tell us, first subjects and second subjects, free fantasias, recapitulations, and codas; there are fugues, with counter−subjects, strettos, and pedal points; there are passacaglias on ground basses, canons ad hypodiapente, and other ingenuities, which have, after all, stood or fallen by their prettiness as much as the

8

simplest folk-tune. Wagner is never driving at anything of this sort any more than Shakespeare in his plays is driving at such ingenuities of verse-making as sonnets, triolets, and the like. And this is why he is so easy for the natural musician who has had no academic teaching. The professors, when Wagner's music is played to them, exclaim at once "What is this? Is it aria, or recitative? Is there no cabaletta to it—not even a full close? Why was that discord not prepared; and why does he not resolve it correctly? How dare he indulge in those scandalous and illicit transitions into a key that has not one note in common with the key he has just left? Listen to those false relations! What does he want with six drums and eight horns when Mozart worked miracles with two of each? The man is no musician." The layman neither knows nor cares about any of these things. If Wagner were to turn aside from his straightforward dramatic purpose to propitiate the professors with correct exercises in sonata form, his music would at once become unintelligible to the unsophisticated spectator, upon whom the familiar and dreaded "classical" sensation would descend like the influenza. Nothing of the kind need be dreaded. The unskilled, untaught musician may approach Wagner boldly; for there is no possibility of a misunderstanding between them: The Ring music is perfectly single and simple. It is the adept musician of the old school who has everything to unlearn: and him I leave, unpitied, to his fate.

THE RING OF THE NIBLUNGS

The Ring consists of four plays, intended to be performed on four successive evenings, entitled The Rhine Gold (a prologue to the other three), The Valkyries, Siegfried, and Night Falls On The Gods; or, in the original German, Das Rheingold, Die Walkure, Siegfried, and Die Gotterdammerung.

THE RHINE GOLD

Let me assume for a moment that you are a young and good-looking woman. Try to imagine yourself in that character at Klondyke five years ago. The place is teeming with gold. If you are content to leave the gold alone, as the wise leave flowers without plucking them, enjoying with perfect naivete its color and glitter and preciousness, no human being will ever be the worse for your knowledge of it; and whilst you remain in that frame of mind the golden age will endure.

Now suppose a man comes along: a man who has no sense of the golden age, nor any power of living in the present: a man with common desires, cupidities, ambitions, just like most of the men you know. Suppose you reveal to that man the fact that if he will only pluck this gold up, and turn it into money, millions of men, driven by the invisible whip of hunger, will toil underground and overground night and day to pile up more and more gold for him until he is master of the world! You will find that the prospect will not tempt him so much as you might imagine, because it involves some distasteful trouble to himself to start with, and because there is something else within his reach involving no distasteful toil, which he desires more passionately; and that is yourself. So long as he is preoccupied with love of you, the gold, and all that it implies, will escape him: the golden age will endure. Not until he forswears love will he stretch out his hand to the gold, and found the Plutonic empire for himself. But the choice between love and gold may not rest altogether with him. He may be an ugly, ungracious, unamiable person, whose affections may seem merely ludicrous and despicable to you. In that case, you may repulse him, and most bitterly humiliate and disappoint him. What is left to him then but to curse the love he can never win, and turn remorselessly to the gold? With that, he will make short work of your golden age, and leave you lamenting its lost thoughtlessness and sweetness.

In due time the gold of Klondyke will find its way to the great cities of the world. But the old dilemma will keep continually reproducing itself. The man who will turn his back on love, and upon all the fruitful it, and will set himself single–heartedly to gather gold in an exultant dream of wielding its Plutonic powers, will find the treasure yielding quickly to his touch. But few men will make this sacrifice voluntarily. Not until the Plutonic power is so strongly set up that the higher human impulses are suppressed as rebellious, and even the mere appetites are denied, starved, and insulted when they cannot purchase their satisfaction with gold, are the energetic spirits driven to build their lives upon riches. How inevitable that course has become to us is plain enough to those who have the power of understanding what they see as they look at the plutocratic societies of our modern capitals.

First Scene

Here, then, is the subject of the first scene of The Rhine Gold. As you sit waiting for the curtain to rise, you suddenly catch the booming ground–tone of a mighty river. It becomes plainer, clearer: you get nearer to the surface, and catch the green light and the flights of bubbles. Then the curtain goes up and you see what you heard—the depths of the Rhine, with three strange fairy fishes, half water–maidens, singing and enjoying themselves exuberantly. They are not singing barcarolles or ballads about the Lorely and her fated lovers, but simply trolling any nonsense that comes into their heads in time to the dancing of the water and the rhythm of their swimming. It is the golden age; and the attraction of this spot for the Rhine maidens is a lump of the Rhine gold, which they value, in an entirely uncommercial way, for its bodily beauty and splendor. Just at present it is eclipsed, because the sun is not striking down through the water.

Presently there comes a poor devil of a dwarf stealing along the slippery rocks of the river bed, a creature with energy enough to make him strong of body and fierce of passion, but with a brutish narrowness of intelligence and selfishness of imagination: too stupid to see that his own welfare can only be compassed as part of the welfare of the world, too full of brute force not to grab vigorously at his own gain. Such dwarfs are quite common in London. He comes now with a fruitful impulse in him, in search of what he lacks in himself, beauty, lightness of heart, imagination, music. The Rhine maidens, representing all these to him, fill him with hope and longing; and he never considers that he has nothing to offer that they could possibly desire, being by natural limitation incapable of seeing anything from anyone else's point of view. With perfect simplicity, he offers himself as a sweetheart to them. But they are thoughtless, elemental, only half real things, much like modern young ladies. That the poor dwarf is repulsive to their sense of physical beauty and their romantic conception of heroism, that he is ugly and awkward, greedy and ridiculous, disposes for them of his claim to live and love. They mock him atrociously, pretending to fall in love with him at first sight, and then slipping away and making game of him, heaping ridicule and disgust on the poor wretch until he is beside himself with mortification and rage. They forget him when the water begins to glitter in the sun, and the gold to reflect its glory. They break into ecstatic worship of their treasure; and though they know the parable of Klondyke quite well, they have no fear that the gold will be wrenched away by the dwarf, since it will yield to no one who has not forsworn love for it, and it is in pursuit of love that he has come to them. They forget that they have poisoned that desire in him by their mockery and denial of it, and that he now knows that life will give him nothing that he cannot wrest from it by the Plutonic power. It is just as if some poor, rough, vulgar, coarse fellow were to offer to take his part in aristocratic society, and be snubbed into the knowledge that only as a millionaire could he ever hope to bring that society to his feet and buy himself a beautiful and refined wife. His choice is forced on him. He forswears love as thousands of us forswear it every day; and in a moment the gold is in his grasp, and he disappears in the depths, leaving the water—fairies vainly screaming "Stop thief!" whilst the river seems to plunge into darkness and sink from us as we rise to the cloud regions above.

And now, what forces are there in the world to resist Alberic, our dwarf, in his new character of sworn plutocrat? He is soon at work wielding the power of the gold. For his gain, hordes of his fellow—creatures are thenceforth condemned to slave miserably, overground and underground, lashed to their work by the invisible whip of starvation. They never see him, any more than the victims of our "dangerous trades" ever see the shareholders whose power is nevertheless everywhere, driving them to destruction. The very wealth they create with their labor becomes an additional force to impoverish them; for as fast as they make it it slips from their hands into the hands of their master, and makes him mightier than ever. You can see the process for yourself in every civilized country today, where millions of people toil in want and disease to heap up more wealth for our Alberics, laying up nothing for themselves, except sometimes horrible and agonizing disease and the certainty of premature death. All this part of the story is frightfully real, frightfully present, frightfully modern; and its effects on our social life are so ghastly and ruinous that we no longer know enough of happiness to be discomposed by it. It is only the poet, with his vision of what life might be, to whom these things are unendurable. If we were a race of poets we would make an end of them before the end of this miserable century. Being a race of moral dwarfs instead, we think them highly respectable, comfortable and proper, and allow them to breed and multiply their evil in all directions. If there were no higher power in the world to work against Alberic, the end of it would be utter destruction.

Such a force there is, however; and it is called Godhead. The mysterious thing we call life organizes itself into all living shapes, bird, beast, beetle and fish, rising to the human marvel in cunning dwarfs and in laborious muscular giants, capable, these last, of enduring toil, willing to buy love and life, not with suicidal curses and renunciations, but with patient manual drudgery in the service of higher powers. And these higher powers are called into existence by the same selforganization of life still more wonderfully into rare persons who may by comparison be called gods, creatures capable of thought, whose aims extend far beyond the satisfaction of their bodily appetites and personal affections, since they perceive that it is only by the establishment of a social order founded on common bonds of moral faith that the world can rise from mere savagery. But how is this order to be set up by Godhead in a world of stupid giants, since these thoughtless ones pursue only their narrower personal ends and can by no means understand the aims of a god? Godhead, face to face with Stupidity, must compromise. Unable to enforce on the world the pure law of thought, it must resort to a mechanical law of commandments to be enforced by brute punishments and the destruction of the disobedient. And however carefully these laws are framed to represent the highest thoughts of the framers at the moment of their promulgation, before a day has elapsed that thought has grown and widened by the ceaseless evolution of life; and lo! yesterday's law already fallen out with today's thought. Yet if the high givers of that law themselves set the example of breaking it before it is a week old, they destroy all its authority with their subjects, and so break the weapon they have forged to rule them for their own good. They must therefore maintain at all costs the sanctity of the law, even when it has ceased to represent their thought; so that at last they get entangled in a network of ordinances which they no longer believe in, and yet have made so sacred by custom and so terrible by punishment, that they cannot themselves escape from them. Thus Godhead's resort to law finally costs it half its integrity—as if a spiritual king, to gain temporal power, had plucked out one of his eyes—and it finally begins secretly to long for the advent of some power higher than itself which will destroy its artificial empire of law, and establish a true republic of free thought.

This is by no means the only difficulty in the dominion of Law. The brute force for its execution must be purchased; and the mass of its subjects must be persuaded to respect the authority which employs this force. But how is such respect to be implanted in them if they are unable to comprehend the thought of the lawgiver? Clearly, only by associating the legislative power with such displays of splendor and majesty as will impress their senses and awe their imaginations. The god turned lawgiver, in short, must be crowned Pontiff and King. Since he cannot be known to the common folk as their superior in wisdom, he must be known to them as their superior in riches, as the dweller in castles, the wearer of gold and purple, the eater of mighty feasts, the commander of armies, and the wielder of powers of life and death, of salvation and damnation after death. Something may be done in this way without corruption whilst the golden age still endures. Your gods may not prevail with the dwarfs; but they may go to these honest giants who will give a day's work for a day's pay, and induce them to build for Godhead a mighty fortress, complete with hall and chapel, tower and bell, for the sake of the homesteads that will grow up in security round that church–castle. This only, however, whilst the golden age lasts. The moment the Plutonic power is let loose, and the loveless Alberic comes into the field with his corrupting millions, the gods are face to face with destruction; since Alberic, able with invisible hunger–whip to force the labor of the dwarfs and to buy the services of the giants, can outshine all the temporal shows and splendors of the golden age, and make himself master of the world, unless the gods, with their bigger brains, can capture his gold. This, the dilemma of the Church today, is the situation created by the exploit of Alberic in the depths of the Rhine.

Second Scene

From the bed of the river we rise into cloudy regions, and finally come out into the clear in a meadow, where Wotan, the god of gods, and his consort Fricka lie sleeping. Wotan, you will observe, has lost one eye; and you will presently learn that he plucked it out voluntarily as the price to be paid for his alliance with Fricka, who in return has brought to him as her dowry all the powers of Law. The meadow is on the brink of a ravine, beyond which, towering on distant heights, stands Godhome, a mighty castle, newly built as a house of state for the one−eyed god and his all−ruling wife. Wotan has not yet seen this castle except in his dreams: two giants have just built it for him whilst he slept; and the reality is before him for the first time when Fricka wakes him. In that majestic burg he is to rule with her and through her over the humble giants, who have eyes to gape at the glorious castles their own hands have built from his design, but no brains to design castles for themselves, or to comprehend divinity. As a god, he is to be great, secure, and mighty; but he is also to be passionless, affectionless, wholly impartial; for Godhead, if it is to live with Law, must have no weaknesses, no respect for persons. All such sweet littlenesses must be left to the humble stupid giants to make their toil sweet to them; and the god must, after all, pay for Olympian power the same price the dwarf has paid for Plutonic power.

Wotan has forgotten this in his dreams of greatness. Not so Fricka. What she is thinking of is this price that Wotan has consented to pay, in token whereof he has promised this day to hand over to the giants Fricka's sister, the goddess Freia, with her golden love−apples. When Fricka reproaches Wotan with having selfishly forgotten this, she finds that he, like herself, is not prepared to go through with his bargain, and that he is trusting to another great worldforce, the Lie (a European Power, as Lassalle said), to help him to trick the giants out of their reward. But this force does not dwell in Wotan himself, but in another, a god over whom he has triumphed, one Loki, the god of Intellect, Argument, Imagination, Illusion, and Reason. Loki has promised to deliver him from his contract, and to cheat the giants for him; but he has not arrived to keep his word: indeed, as Fricka bitterly points out, why should not the Lie fail Wotan, since such failure is the very essence of him?

The giants come soon enough; and Freia flies to Wotan for protection against them. Their purposes are quite honest; and they have no doubt of the god's faith. There stands their part of the contract fulfilled, stone on stone, port and pinnacle all faithfully finished from Wotan's design by their mighty labor. They have come undoubtingly for their agreed wage. Then there happens what is to them an incredible, inconceivable thing. The god begins to shuffle. There are no moments in life more tragic than those in which the humble common man, the manual worker, leaving with implicit trust all high affairs to his betters, and reverencing them wholly as worthy of that trust, even to the extent of accepting as his rightful function the saving of them from all roughening and coarsening drudgeries, first discovers that they are corrupt, greedy, unjust and treacherous. The shock drives a ray of prophetic light into one giant's mind, and gives him a momentary eloquence. In that moment he rises above his stupid gianthood, and earnestly warns the Son of Light that all his power and eminence of priesthood, godhood, and kingship must stand or fall with the unbearable cold greatness of the incorruptible law–giver. But Wotan, whose assumed character of law–giver is altogether false to his real passionate nature, despises the rebuke; and the giant's ray of insight is lost in the murk of his virtuous indignation.

In the midst of the wrangle, Loki comes at last, excusing himself for being late on the ground that he has been detained by a matter of importance which he has promised to lay before Wotan. When pressed to give his mind to the business immediately in hand, and to extricate Wotan from his dilemma, he has nothing to say except that the giants are evidently altogether in the right. The castle has been duly built: he has tried every stone of it, and found the work first–rate: there is nothing to be done but pay the price agreed upon by handing over Freia to the giants. The gods are furious; and Wotan passionately declares that he only consented to the bargain on Loki's promise to find a way for him out of it. But Loki says no: he has promised to find a way out if any such way exist, but not to make a way if there is no way. He has wandered over the whole earth in search of some treasure great enough to buy Freia back from the giants; but in all the world he has found nothing for which Man will give up Woman. And this, by the way, reminds him of the matter he had promised to lay before Wotan. The Rhine maidens have complained to him of Alberic's theft of their gold; and he mentions it as a curious exception to his universal law of the unpurchasable preciousness of love, that this gold–robber has forsworn love for the sake of the fabulous riches of the Plutonic empire and the mastery of the world through its power.

No sooner is the tale told than the giants stoop lower than the dwarf. Alberic forswore love only when it was denied to him and made the instrument for cruelly murdering his self—respect. But the giants, with love within their reach, with Freia and her golden apples in their hands, offer to give her up for the treasure of Alberic. Observe, it is the treasure alone that they desire. They have no fierce dreams of dominion over their superiors, or of moulding the world to any conceptions of their own. They are neither clever nor ambitious: they simply covet money. Alberic's gold: that is their demand, or else Freia, as agreed upon, whom they now carry off as hostage, leaving Wotan to consider their ultimatum.

Freia gone, the gods begin to wither and age: her golden apples, which they so lightly bargained away, they now find to be a matter of life and death to them; for not even the gods can live on Law and Godhead alone, be their castles ever so splendid. Loki alone is unaffected: the Lie, with all its cunning wonders, its glistenings and shiftings and mirages, is a mere appearance: it has no body and needs no food. What is Wotan to do? Loki sees the answer clearly enough: he must bluntly rob Alberic. There is nothing to prevent him except moral scruple; for Alberic, after all, is a poor, dim, dwarfed, credulous creature whom a god can outsee and a lie can outwit. Down, then, Wotan and Loki plunge into the mine where Alberic's slaves are piling up wealth for him under the invisible whip.

Third Scene

This gloomy place need not be a mine: it might just as well be a match—factory, with yellow phosphorus, phossy jaw, a large dividend, and plenty of clergymen shareholders. Or it might be a whitelead factory, or a chemical works, or a pottery, or a railway shunting yard, or a tailoring shop, or a little gin—sodden laundry, or a bakehouse, or a big shop, or any other of the places where human life and welfare are daily sacrificed in order that some greedy foolish creature may be able to hymn exultantly to his Platonic idol:

Thou mak'st me eat whilst others starve, And sing while others do lament: Such untome Thy blessings are, As if I were Thine only care.

In the mine, which resounds with the clinking anvils of the dwarfs toiling miserably to heap up treasure for their master, Alberic has set his brother Mime—more familiarly, Mimmy—to make him a helmet. Mimmy dimly sees that there is some magic in this helmet, and tries to keep it; but Alberic wrests it from him, and shows him, to his cost, that it is the veil of the invisible whip, and that he who wears it can appear in what shape he will, or disappear from view altogether. This helmet is a very common article in our streets, where it generally takes the form of a tall hat. It makes a man invisible as a shareholder, and changes him into various shapes, such as a pious Christian, a subscriber to hospitals, a benefactor of the poor, a model husband and father, a shrewd, practical independent Englishman, and what not, when he is really a pitiful parasite on the commonwealth, consuming a great deal, and producing nothing, feeling nothing, knowing nothing, believing nothing, and doing nothing except what all the rest do, and that only because he is afraid not to do it, or at least pretend to do it.

When Wotan and Loki arrive, Loki claims Alberic as an old acquaintance. But the dwarf has no faith in these civil strangers: Greed instinctively mistrusts Intellect, even in the garb of Poetry and the company of Godhead, whilst envying the brilliancy of the one and the dignity of the other. Alberic breaks out at them with a terrible boast of the power now within his grasp. He paints for them the world as it will be when his dominion over it is complete, when the soft airs and green mosses of its valleys shall be changed into smoke, slag, and filth; when slavery, disease, and squalor, soothed by drunkenness and mastered by the policeman's baton, shall become the foundation of society; and when nothing shall escape ruin except such pretty places and pretty women as he may like to buy for the slaking of his own lusts. In that kingdom of evil he sees that there will be no power but his own. These gods, with their moralities and legalities and intellectual subtlety, will go under and be starved out of existence. He bids Wotan and Loki beware of it; and his "Hab' Acht!" is hoarse, horrible, and sinister. Wotan is revolted to the very depths of his being: he cannot stifle the execration that bursts from him. But Loki is unaffected: he has no moral passion: indignation is as absurd to him as enthusiasm. He finds it exquisitely amusing—having a touch of the comic spirit in him—that the dwarf, in stirring up the moral fervor of Wotan, has removed his last moral scruple about becoming a thief. Wotan will now rob the dwarf without remorse; for is it not positively his highest duty to take this power out of such evil hands and use it himself in the interests of Godhead? On the loftiest moral grounds, he lets Loki do his worst.

A little cunningly disguised flattery makes short work of Alberic. Loki pretends to be afraid of him; and he swallows that bait unhesitatingly. But how, enquires Loki, is he to guard against the hatred of his million slaves? Will they not steal from him, whilst he sleeps, the magic ring, the symbol of his power, which he has forged from the gold of the Rhine? "You think yourself very clever," sneers Alberic, and then begins to boast of the enchantments of the magic helmet. Loki refuses to believe in such marvels without witnessing them. Alberic, only too glad to show off his powers, puts on the helmet and transforms himself into a monstrous serpent. Loki gratifies him by pretending to be frightened out of his wits, but ventures to remark that it would be better still if the helmet could transform its owner into some tiny creature that could hide and spy in the smallest cranny. Alberic promptly transforms himself into a toad. In an instant Wotan's foot is on him; Loki tears away the helmet; they pinion him, and drag him away a prisoner up through the earth to the meadow by the castle.

Fourth Scene

There, to pay for his freedom, he has to summon his slaves from the depths to place all the treasure they have heaped up for him at the feet of Wotan. Then he demands his liberty; but Wotan must have the ring as well. And here the dwarf, like the giant before him, feels the very foundations of the world shake beneath him at the discovery of his own base cupidity in a higher power. That evil should, in its loveless desperation, create malign powers which Godhead could not create, seems but natural justice to him. But that Godhead should steal those malign powers from evil, and wield them itself, is a monstrous perversion; and his appeal to Wotan to forego it is almost terrible in its conviction of wrong. It is of no avail. Wotan falls back again on virtuous indignation. He reminds Alberic that he stole the gold from the Rhine maidens, and takes the attitude of the just judge compelling a restitution of stolen goods. Alberic knowing perfectly well that the judge is taking the goods to put them m his own pocket, has the ring torn from his finger, and is once more as poor as he was when he came slipping and stumbling among the slimy rocks in the bed of the Rhine.

This is the way of the world. In older times, when the Christian laborer was drained dry by the knightly spendthrift, and the spendthrift was drained by the Jewish usurer, Church and State, religion and law, seized on the Jew and drained him as a Christian duty. When the forces of lovelessness and greed had built up our own sordid capitalist systems, driven by invisible proprietorship, robbing the poor, defacing the earth, and forcing themselves as a universal curse even on the generous and humane, then religion and law and intellect, which would never themselves have discovered such systems, their natural bent being towards welfare, economy, and life instead of towards corruption, waste, and death, nevertheless did not scruple to seize by fraud and force these powers of evil on presence of using them for good. And it inevitably happens that when the Church, the Law, and all the Talents have made common cause to rob the people, the Church is far more vitally harmed by that unfaithfulness to itself than its more mechanical confederates; so that finally they turn on their discredited ally and rob the Church, with the cheerful co—operation of Loki, as in France and Italy for instance.

The twin giants come back with their hostage, in whose presence Godhead blooms again. The gold is ready for them; but now that the moment has come for parting with Freia the gold does not seem so tempting; and they are sorely loth to let her go. Not unless there is gold enough to utterly hide her from them—not until the heap has grown so that they can see nothing but gold—until money has come between them and every human feeling, will they part with her. There is not gold enough to accomplish this: however cunningly Loki spreads it, the glint of Freia's hair is still visible to Giant Fafnir, and the magic helmet must go on the heap to shut it out. Even then Fafnir's brother, Fasolt, can catch a beam from her eye through a chink, and is rendered incapable thereby of forswearing her. There is nothing to stop that chink but the ring; and Wotan is as greedily bent on keeping that as Alberic himself was; nor can the other gods persuade him that Freia is worth it, since for the highest god, love is not the highest good, but only the universal delight that bribes all living things to travail with renewed life. Life itself, with its accomplished marvels and its infinite potentialities, is the only force that Godhead can worship. Wotan does not yield until he is reached by the voice of the fruitful earth that before he or the dwarfs or the giants or the Law or the Lie or any of these things were, had the seed of them all in her bosom, and the seed perhaps of something higher even than himself, that shall one day supersede him and cut the tangles and alliances and compromises that already have cost him one of his eyes. When Erda, the First Mother of life, rises from her sleeping—place in the heart of the earth, and warns him to yield the ring, he obeys her; the ring is added to the heap of gold; and all sense of Freia is cut off from the giants.

But now what Law is left to these two poor stupid laborers whereby one shall yield to the other any of the treasure for which they have each paid the whole price in surrendering Freia? They look by mere habit to the god to judge for them; but he, with his heart stirring towards higher forces than himself, turns with disgust from these lower forces.

They settle it as two wolves might; and Fafnir batters his brother dead with his staff. It is a horrible thing to see and hear, to anyone who knows how much blood has been shed in the world in just that way by its brutalized toilers, honest fellows enough until their betters betrayed them. Fafnir goes off with his booty. It is quite useless to him. He has neither the cunning nor the ambition to establish the Plutonic empire with it. Merely to prevent others from getting it is the only purpose it brings him. He piles it in a cave; transforms himself into a dragon by the helmet; and devotes his life to guarding it, as much a slave to it as a jailor is to his prisoner. He had much better have thrown it all back into the Rhine and transformed himself into the shortest–lived animal that enjoys at least a brief run in the sunshine. His case, however, is far too common to be surprising. The world is overstocked with persons who sacrifice all their affections, and madly trample and batter down their fellows to obtain riches of which, when they get them, they are unable to make the smallest use, and to which they become the most miserable slaves.

The gods soon forget Fafnir in their rejoicing over Freia. Donner, the Thunder god, springs to a rocky summit and calls the clouds as a shepherd calls his flocks. They come at his summons; and he and the castle are hidden by their black legions. Froh, the Rainbow god, hastens to his side. At the stroke of Donner's hammer the black murk is riven in all directions by darting ribbons of lightning; and as the air clears, the castle is seen m its fullest splendor, accessible now by the rainbow bridge which Froh has cast across the ravine. In the glory of this moment Wotan has a great thought. With all his aspirations to establish a reign of noble thought, of righteousness, order, and justice, he has found that day that there is no race yet in the world that quite spontaneously, naturally, and unconsciously realizes his ideal. He himself has found how far short Godhead falls of the thing it conceives. He, the greatest of gods, has been unable to control his fate: he has been forced against his will to choose between evils, to make disgraceful bargains, to break them still more disgracefully, and even then to see the price of his disgrace slip through his fingers. His consort has cost him half his vision; his castle has cost him his affections; and the attempt to retain both has cost him his honor. On every side he is shackled and bound, dependent on the laws of Fricka and on the lies of Loki, forced to traffic with dwarfs for handicraft and with giants for strength, and to pay them both in false coin. After all, a god is a pitiful thing. But the fertility of the First Mother is not yet exhausted. The life that came from her has ever climbed up to a higher and higher organization. From toad and serpent to dwarf, from bear and elephant to giant, from dwarf and giant to a god with thoughts, with comprehension of the world, with ideals. Why should it stop there? Why should it not rise from the god to the Hero? to the creature in whom the god's unavailing thought shall have become effective will and life, who shall make his way straight to truth and reality over the laws of Fricka and the lies of Loki with a strength that overcomes giants and a cunning that outwits dwarfs? Yes: Erda, the First Mother, must travail again, and breed him a race of heroes to deliver the world and himself from his limited powers and disgraceful bargains. This is the vision that flashes on him as he turns to the rainbow bridge and calls his wife to come and dwell with him in Valhalla, the home of the gods.

They are all overcome with Valhalla's glory except Loki. He is behind the scenes of this joint reign of the Divine and the Legal. He despises these gods with their ideals and their golden apples. "I am ashamed," he says, "to have dealings with these futile creatures." And so he follows them to the rainbow bridge. But as they set foot on it, from the river below rises the wailing of the Rhine maidens for their lost gold. "You down there in the water," cries Loki with brutal irony: "you used to bask in the glitter of your gold: henceforth you shall bask in the splendor of the gods." And they reply that the truth is in the depths and the darkness, and that what blazes on high there is falsehood. And with that the gods pass into their glorious stronghold.

WAGNER AS REVOLUTIONIST

Before leaving this explanation of The Rhine Gold, I must have a word or two about it with the reader. It is the least popular of the sections of The Ring. The reason is that its dramatic moments lie quite outside the consciousness of people whose joys and sorrows are all domestic and personal, and whose religions and political ideas are purely conventional and superstitious. To them it is a struggle between half a dozen fairytale personages for a ring, involving hours of scolding and cheating, and one long scene in a dark gruesome mine, with gloomy, ugly music, and not a glimpse of a handsome young man or pretty woman. Only those of wider consciousness can follow it breathlessly, seeing in it the whole tragedy of human history and the whole horror of the dilemmas from which the world is shrinking today. At Bayreuth I have seen a party of English tourists, after enduring agonies of boredom from Alberic, rise in the middle of the third scene, and almost force their way out of the dark theatre into the sunlit pine-wood without. And I have seen people who were deeply affected by the scene driven almost beside themselves by this disturbance. But it was a very natural thing for the unfortunate tourists to do, since in this Rhine Gold prologue there is no interval between the acts for escape. Roughly speaking, people who have no general ideas, no touch of the concern of the philosopher and statesman for the race, cannot enjoy The Rhine Gold as a drama. They may find compensations in some exceedingly pretty music, at times even grand and glorious, which will enable them to escape occasionally from the struggle between Alberic and Wotan; but if their capacity for music should be as limited as their comprehension of the world, they had better stay away.

And now, attentive Reader, we have reached the point at which some foolish person is sure to interrupt us by declaring that The Rhine Gold is what they call "a work of art" pure and simple, and that Wagner never dreamt of shareholders, tall hats, whitelead factories, and industrial and political questions looked at from the socialistic and humanitarian points of view. We need not discuss these impertinences: it is easier to silence them with the facts of Wagner's life. In 1843 he obtained the position of conductor of the Opera at Dresden at a salary of L225 a year, with a pension. This was a first-rate permanent appointment in the service of the Saxon State, carrying an assured professional position and livelihood with it In 1848, the year of revolutions, the discontented middle class, unable to rouse the Churchand-State governments of the day from their bondage to custom, caste, and law by appeals to morality or constitutional agitation for Liberal reforms, made common cause with the starving wage-working class, and resorted to armed rebellion, which reached Dresden in 1849. Had Wagner been the mere musical epicure and political mugwump that the term "artist" seems to suggest to so many critics and amateurs—that is, a creature in their own lazy likeness—he need have taken no more part in the political struggles of his day than Bishop took in the English Reform agitation of 1832, or Sterndale Bennett in the Chartist or Free Trade movements. What he did do was first to make a desperate appeal to the King to cast off his bonds and answer the need of the time by taking true Kingship on himself and leading his people to the redress of their intolerable wrongs (fancy the poor monarch's feelings!), and then, when the crash came, to take his side with the right and the poor against the rich and the wrong. When the insurrection was defeated, three leaders of it were especially marked down for vengeance: August Roeckel, an old friend of Wagner's to whom he wrote a well-known series of letters; Michael Bakoonin, afterwards a famous apostle of revolutionary Anarchism; and Wagner himself. Wagner escaped to Switzerland: Roeckel and Bakoonin suffered long terms of imprisonment. Wagner was of course utterly ruined, pecuniarily and socially (to his own intense relief and satisfaction); and his exile lasted twelve years. His first idea was to get his Tannhauser produced in Paris. With the notion of explaining himself to the Parisians he wrote a pamphlet entitled Art and Revolution, a glance through which will show how thoroughly the socialistic side of the revolution had his sympathy, and how completely he had got free from the influence of the established Churches of his day. For three years he kept pouring forth pamphlets—some of them elaborate treatises in size and intellectual rank, but still essentially the pamphlets and manifestoes of a born agitator—on social evolution, religion, life, art and the influence of riches. In 1853 the poem of The Ring was privately printed; and in 1854, five years after the Dresden insurrection, The Rhine Gold score was completed to the last drum tap.

These facts are on official record in Germany, where the proclamation summing up Wagner as "a politically dangerous person" may be consulted to this day. The pamphlets are now accessible to English readers in the translation of Mr. Ashton Ellis. This being so, any person who, having perhaps heard that I am a Socialist, attempts to persuade you that my interpretation of The Rhine Gold is only "my socialism" read into the works of a dilettantist who borrowed an idle tale from an old saga to make an opera book with, may safely be dismissed from your consideration as an ignoramus.

If you are now satisfied that The Rhine Gold is an allegory, do not forget that an allegory is never quite consistent except when it is written by someone without dramatic faculty, in which case it is unreadable. There is only one way of dramatizing an idea; and that is by puttmg on the stage a human being possessed by that idea, yet none the less a human being with all the human impulses which make him akin and therefore interesting to us. Bunyan, in his Pilgrim's Progress, does not, like his unread imitators, attempt to personify Christianity and Valour: he dramatizes for you the life of the Christian and the Valiant Man. Just so, though I have shown that Wotan is Godhead and Kingship, and Loki Logic and Imagination without living Will (Brain without Heart, to put it vulgarly); yet in the drama Wotan is a religiously moral man, and Loki a witty, ingenious, imaginative and cynical one. As to Fricka, who stands for State Law, she does not assume her allegorical character in The Rhine Gold at all, but is simply Wotan's wife and Freia's sister: nay, she contradicts her allegorical self by conniving at all Wotan's rogueries. That, of course, is just what State Law would do; but we must not save the credit of the allegory by a quip. Not until she reappears in the next play (The Valkyries) does her function in the allegorical scheme become plain.

One preconception will bewilder the spectator hopelessly unless he has been warned against it or is naturally free from it. In the old-fashioned orders of creation, the supernatural personages are invariably conceived as greater than man, for good or evil. In the modern humanitarian order as adopted by Wagner, Man is the highest. In The Rhine Gold, it is pretended that there are as yet no men on the earth. There are dwarfs, giants, and gods. The danger is that you will jump to the conclusion that the gods, at least, are a higher order than the human order. On the contrary, the world is waiting for Man to redeem it from the lame and cramped government of the gods. Once grasp that; and the allegory becomes simple enough. Really, of course, the dwarfs, giants, and gods are dramatizations of the three main orders of men: to wit, the instinctive, predatory, lustful, greedy people; the patient, toiling, stupid, respectful, money—worshipping people; and the intellectual, moral, talented people who devise and administer States and Churches. History shows us only one order higher than the highest of these: namely, the order of Heroes.

Now it is quite clear—though you have perhaps never thought of it—that if the next generation of Englishmen consisted wholly of Julius Caesars, all our political, ecclesiastical, and moral institutions would vanish, and the less perishable of their appurtenances be classed with Stonehenge and the cromlechs and round towers as inexplicable relics of a bygone social order. Julius Caesars would no more trouble themselves about such contrivances as our codes and churches than a fellow of the Royal Society will touch his hat to the squire and listen to the village curate's sermons. This is precisely what must happen some day if life continues thrusting towards higher and higher organization as it has hitherto done. As most of our English professional men are to Australian bushmen, so, we must suppose, will the average man of some future day be to Julius Caesar. Let any man of middle age, pondering this prospect consider what has happened within a single generation to the articles of faith his father regarded as eternal nay, to the very scepticisms and blasphemies of his youth (Bishop Colenso's criticism of the Pentateuch, for example!); and he will begin to realize how much of our barbarous Theology and Law the man of the future will do without. Bakoonin, the Dresden revolutionary leader with whom Wagner went out in 1849, put forward later on a program, often quoted with foolish horror, for the abolition of all institutions, religious, political, juridical, financial, legal, academic, and so on, so as to leave the will of man free to find its own way. All the loftiest spirits of that time were burning to raise Man up, to give him self—respect, to shake him out of his habit of grovelling before the ideals created by his own imagination, of attributmg the good that sprang from the ceaseless energy of the life within himself to some superior power in the clouds, and of making a fetish of self—sacrifice to justify his own cowardice.

Farther on in The Ring we shall see the Hero arrive and make an end of dwarfs, giants, and gods. Meanwhile, let us not forget that godhood means to Wagner infirmity and compromise, and manhood strength and integrity. Above all, we must understand— for it is the key to much that we are to see—that the god, since his desire is toward a higher and fuller life, must long in his inmost soul for the advent of that greater power whose first work, though this he does not see as yet, must be his own undoing.

In the midst of all these far–reaching ideas, it is amusing to find Wagner still full of his ingrained theatrical professionalism, and introducing effects which now seem old–fashioned and stagey with as much energy and earnestness as if they were his loftiest inspirations. When Wotan wrests the ring from Alberic, the dwarf delivers a lurid and bloodcurdling stage curse, calling down on its every future possessor care, fear, and death. The musical phrase accompanying this outburst was a veritable harmonic and melodic bogey to mid–century ears, though time has now robbed it of its terrors. It sounds again when Fafnir slays Fasolt, and on every subsequent occasion when the ring brings death to its holder. This episode must justify itself purely as a piece of stage sensationalism. On deeper ground it is superfluous and confusing, as the ruin to which the pursuit of riches leads needs no curse to explain it; nor is there any sense in investing Alberic with providential powers in the matter.

THE VALKYRIES

Before the curtain rises on the Valkyries, let us see what has happened since it fell on The Rhine Gold. The persons of the drama will tell us presently; but as we probably do not understand German, that may not help us.

Wotan is still ruling the world in glory from his giantbuilt castle with his wife Fricka. But he has no security for the continuance of his reign, since Alberic may at any moment contrive to recover the ring, the full power of which he can wield because he has forsworn love. Such forswearing is not possible to Wotan: love, though not his highest need, is a higher than gold: otherwise he would be no god. Besides, as we have seen, his power has been established in the world by and as a system of laws enforced by penalties. These he must consent to be bound by himself; for a god who broke his own laws would betray the fact that legality and conformity are not the highest rule of conduct—a discovery fatal to his supremacy as Pontiff and Lawgiver. Hence "he may not wrest the ring unlawfully from Fafnir, even if he could bring himself to forswear love.

In this insecurity he has hit on the idea of forming a heroic bodyguard. He has trained his love children as war–maidens (Valkyries) whose duty it is to sweep through battle–fields and bear away to Valhalla the souls of the bravest who fall there. Thus reinforced by a host of warriors, he has thoroughly indoctrinated them, Loki helping him as dialectician–in–chief, with the conventional system of law and duty, supernatural religion and self–sacrificing idealism, which they believe to be the essence of his godhood, but which is really only the machinery of the love of necessary power which is his mortal weakness. This process secures their fanatical devotion to his system of government, but he knows perfectly well that such systems, in spite of their moral pretensions, serve selfish and ambitious tyrants better than benevolent despots, and that, if once Alberic gets the ring back, he will easily out–Valhalla Valhalla, if not buy it over as a going concern. The only chance of permanent security, then, is the appearance in the world of a hero who, without any illicit prompting from Wotan, will destroy Alberic and wrest the ring from Fafnir. There will then, he believes, be no further cause for anxiety, since he does not yet conceive Heroism as a force hostile to Godhead. In his longing for a rescuer, it does not occur to him that when the Hero comes, his first exploit must be to sweep the gods and their ordinances from the path of the heroic will.

Indeed, he feels that in his own Godhead is the germ of such Heroism, and that from himself the Hero must spring. He takes to wandering, mostly in search of love, from Fricka and Valhalla. He seeks the First Mother; and through her womb, eternally fertile, the inner true thought that made him first a god is reborn as his daughter, uncorrupted by his ambition, unfettered by his machinery of power and his alliances with Fricka and Loki. This daughter, the Valkyrie Brynhild, is his true will, his real self, (as he thinks): to her he may say what he must not say to anyone, since in speaking to her he but speaks to himself. "Was Keinem in Worten unausgesprochen," he says to her, "bleib es ewig: mit mir nur rath' ich, red' ich zu dir."

But from Brynhild no hero can spring until there is a man of Wotan's race to breed with her. Wotan wanders further; and a mortal woman bears him twins: a son and a daughter. He separates them by letting the girl fall into the hands of a forest tribe which in due time gives her as a wife to a fierce chief, one Hunding. With the son he himself leads the life of a wolf, and teaches him the only power a god can teach, the power of doing without happiness. When he has given him this terrible training, he abandons him, and goes to the bridal feast of his daughter Sieglinda and Hunding. In the blue cloak of the wanderer, wearing the broad hat that flaps over the socket of his forfeited eye, he appears in Hunding's house, the middle pillar of which is a mighty tree. Into that tree, without a word, he strikes a sword up to the hilt, so that only the might of a hero can withdraw it. Then he goes out as silently as he came, blind to the truth that no weapon from the armory of Godhead can serve the turn of the true Human Hero. Neither Hunding nor any of his guests can move the sword; and there it stays awaiting the destined hand. That is the history of the generations between The Rhine Gold and The Valkyries.

The First Act

This time, as we sit looking expectantly at the curtain, we hear, not the deep booming of the Rhine, but the patter of a forest downpour, accompanied by the mutter of a storm which soon gathers into a roar and culminates in crashing thunderbolts. As it passes off, the curtain rises; and there is no mistaking whose forest habitation we are in; for the central pillar is a mighty tree, and the place fit for the dwelling of a fierce chief. The door opens: and an exhausted man reels in: an adept from the school of unhappiness. Sieglinda finds him lying on the hearth. He explains that he has been in a fight; that his weapons not being as strong as his arms, were broken; and that he had to fly. He desires some drink and a moment's rest; then he will go; for he is an unlucky person, and does not want to bring his ill-luck on the woman who is succoring him. But she, it appears, is also unhappy; and a strong sympathy springs up between them. When her husband arrives, he observes not only this sympathy, but a resemblance between them, a gleam of the snake in their eyes. They sit down to table; and the stranger tells them his unlucky story. He is the son of Wotan, who is known to him only as Wolfing, of the race of the Volsungs. The earliest thing he remembers is returning from a hunt with his father to find their home destroyed, his mother murdered, and his twin-sister carried off. This was the work of a tribe called the Neidings, upon whom he and Wolfing thenceforth waged implacable war until the day when his father disappeared, leaving no trace of himself but an empty wolfskin. The young Volsung was thus cast alone upon the world, finding most hands against him, and bringing no good luck even to his friends. His latest exploit has been the slaying of certain brothers who were forcing their sister to wed against her will. The result has been the slaughter of the woman by her brothers' clansmen, and his own narrow escape by flight.

His luck on this occasion is even worse than he supposes; for Hunding, by whose hearth he has taken refuge, is clansman to the slain brothers and is bound to avenge them. He tells the Volsung that in the morning, weapons or no weapons, he must fight for his life. Then he orders the woman to bed, and follows her himself, taking his spear with him.

The unlucky stranger, left brooding by the hearth, has nothing to console himself with but an old promise of his father's that he shall find a weapon to his hand when he most needs one. The last flicker of the dying fire strikes on the golden hilt of the sword that sticks in the tree; but he does not see it; and the embers sink into blackness. Then the woman returns. Hunding is safely asleep: she has drugged him. She tells the story of the one—eyed man who appeared at her forced marriage, and of the sword. She has always felt, she says, that her miseries will end in the arms of the hero who shall succeed in drawing it forth. The stranger, diffident as he is about his luck, has no misgivings as to his strength and destiny. He gives her his affection at once, and abandons himself to the charm of the night and the season; for it is the beginning of Spring. They soon learn from their confidences that she is his stolen twin—sister. He is transported to find that the heroic race of the Volsungs need neither perish nor be corrupted by a lower strain. Hailing the sword by the name of Nothung (or Needed), he plucks it from the tree as her bride—gift, and then, crying "Both bride and sister be of thy brother; and blossom the blood of the Volsungs!" clasps her as the mate the Spring has brought him.

The Second Act

So far, Wotan's plan seems prospering. In the mountains he calls his war—maiden Brynhild, the child borne to him by the First Mother, and bids her see to it that Hunding shall fall in the approaching combat. But he is reckoning without his consort, Fricka. What will she, the Law, say to the lawless pair who have heaped incest on adultery? A hero may have defied the law, and put his own will in its place; but can a god hold him guiltless, when the whole power of the gods can enforce itself only by law? Fricka, shuddering with horror, outraged in every instinct, comes clamoring for punishment. Wotan pleads the general necessity of encouraging heroism in order to keep up the Valhalla bodyguard; but his remonstrances only bring upon him torrents of reproaches for his own unfaithfulness to the law in roaming through the world and begetting war—maidens, "wolf cubs," and the like. He is hopelessly beaten in the argument. Fricka is absolutely right when she declares that the ending of the gods began when he brought this wolf—hero into the world; and now, to save their very existence, she pitilessly demands his destruction. Wotan has no power to refuse: it is Fricka's mechanical force, and not his thought, that really rules the world. He has to recall Brynhild; take back his former instructions; and ordain that Hunding shall slay the Volsung.

But now comes another difficulty. Brynhild is the inner thought and will of Godhead, the aspiration from the high life to the higher that is its divine element, and only becomes separated from it when its resort to kingship and priestcraft for the sake of temporal power has made it false to itself. Hitherto, Brynhild, as Valkyrie or hero chooser, has obeyed Wotan implicitly, taking her work as the holiest and bravest in his kingdom; and now he tells her what he could not tell Fricka—what indeed he could not tell to Brynhild, were she not, as she says, his own will—the whole story of Alberic and of that inspiration about the raising up of a hero. She thoroughly approves of the inspiration; but when the story ends in the assumption that she too must obey Fricka, and help Fricka's vassal, Hunding, to undo the great work and strike the hero down, she for the first time hesitates to accept his command. In his fury and despair he overawes her by the most terrible threats of his anger; and she submits.

Then comes the Volsung Siegmund, following his sister bride, who has fled into the mountains in a revulsion of horror at having allowed herself to bring her hero to shame. Whilst she is lying exhausted and senseless in his arms, Brynhild appears to him and solemnly warns him that he must presently leave the earth with her. He asks whither he must follow her. To Valhalla, to take his place there among the heroes. He asks, shall he find his father there? Yes. Shall he find a wife there? Yes: he will be waited on by beautiful wishmaidens. Shall he meet his sister there? No. Then, says Siegmund, I will not come with you.

She tries to make him understand that he cannot help himself. Being a hero, he will not be so persuaded: he has his father's sword, and does not fear Hunding. But when she tells him that she comes from his father, and that the sword of a god will not avail in the hands of a hero, he accepts his fate, but will shape it with his own hand, both for himself and his sister, by slaying her, and then killing himself with the last stroke of the sword. And thereafter he will go to Hell, rather than to Valhalla.

How now can Brynhild, being what she is, choose her side freely in a conflict between this hero and the vassal of Fricka? By instinct she at once throws Wotan's command to the winds, and bids Siegmund nerve himself for the combat with Hunding, in which she pledges him the protection of her shield. The horn of Hunding is soon heard; and Siegmund's spirits rise to fighting pitch at once. The two meet; and the Valkyrie's shield is held before the hero. But when he delivers his sword–stroke at his foe, the weapon shivers on the spear of Wotan, who suddenly appears between them; and the first of the race of heroes falls with the weapon of the Law's vassal through his breast. Brynhild snatches the fragments of the broken sword, and flies, carrying off the woman with her on her war–horse; and Wotan, in terrible wrath, slays Hunding with a wave of his hand, and starts in pursuit of his disobedient daughter.

The Third Act

On a rocky peak, four of the Valkyries are waiting for the rest. The absent ones soon arrive, galloping through the air with slain heroes, gathered from the battle–field, hanging over their saddles. Only, Brynhild, who comes last, has for her spoil a live woman. When her eight sisters learn that she has defied Wotan, they dare not help her; and Brynhild has to rouse Sieglinda to make an effort to save herself, by reminding her that she bears in her the seed of a hero, and must face everything, endure anything, sooner than let that seed miscarry. Sieglinda, in a transport of exaltation, takes the fragments of the sword and flies into the forest. Then Wotan comes; the sisters fly in terror at his command; and he is left alone with Brynhild.

Here, then, we have the first of the inevitable moments which Wotan did not foresee. Godhead has now established its dominion over the world by a mighty Church, compelling obedience through its ally the Law, with its formidable State organization of force of arms and cunning of brain. It has submitted to this alliance to keep the Plutonic power in check—built it up primarily for the sake of that soul in itself which cares only to make the highest better and the best higher; and now here is that very soul separated from it and working for the destruction of its indispensable ally, the lawgiving State. How is the rebel to be disarmed? Slain it cannot be by Godhead, since it is still Godhead's own very dearest soul. But hidden, stifled, silenced it must be; or it will wreck the State and leave the Church defenseless. Not until it passes completely away from Godhead, and is reborn as the soul of the hero, can it work anything but the confusion and destruction of the existing order. How is the world to be protected against it in the meantime? Clearly Loki's help is needed here: it is the Lie that must, on the highest principles, hide the Truth. Let Loki surround this mountain top with the appearance of a consuming fire; and who will dare penetrate to Brynhild? It is true that if any man will walk boldly into that fire, he will discover it at once to be a lie, an illusion, a mirage through which he might carry a sack of gunpowder without being a penny the worse. Therefore let the fire seem so terrible that only the hero, when in the fulness of time he appears upon earth, will venture through it; and the problem is solved. Wotan, with a breaking heart, takes leave of Brynhild; throws her into a deep sleep; covers her with her long warshield; summons Loki, who comes in the shape of a wall of fire surrounding the mountain peak; and turns his back on Brynhild for ever.

The allegory here is happily not so glaringly obvious to the younger generations of our educated classes as it was forty years ago. In those days, any child who expressed a doubt as to the absolute truth of the Church's teaching, even to the extent of asking why Joshua told the sun to stand still instead of telling the earth to cease turning, or of pointing out that a whale's throat would hardly have been large enough to swallow Jonah, was unhesitatingly told that if it harboured such doubts it would spend all eternity after its death in horrible torments in a lake of burning brimstone. It is difficult to write or read this nowadays without laughing; yet no doubt millions of ignorant and credulous people are still teaching their children that. When Wagner himself was a little child, the fact that hell was a fiction devised for the intimidation and subjection of the masses, was a well–kept secret of the thinking and governing classes. At that time the fires of Loki were a very real terror to all except persons of exceptional force of character and intrepidity of thought. Even thirty years after Wagner had printed the verses of The Ring for private circulation, we find him excusing himself from perfectly explicit denial of current superstitions, by reminding his readers that it would expose him to prosecution. In England, so many of our respectable voters are still grovelling in a gloomy devil worship, of which the fires of Loki are the main bulwark, that no Government has yet had the conscience or the courage to repeal our monstrous laws against "blasphemy."

SIEGFRIED

Sieglinda, when she flies into the forest with the hero's son unborn in her womb, and the broken pieces of his sword in her hand, finds shelter in the smithy of a dwarf, where she brings forth her child and dies. This dwarf is no other than Mimmy, the brother of Alberic, the same who made for him the magic helmet. His aim in life is to gain possession of the helmet, the ring, and the treasure, and through them to obtain that Plutonic mastery of the world under the beginnings of which he himself writhed during

Alberic's brief reign. Mimmy is a blinking, shambling, ancient creature, too weak and timid to dream of taking arms himself to despoil Fafnir, who still, transformed to a monstrous serpent, broods on the gold in a hole in the rocks. Mimmy needs the help of a hero for that; and he has craft enough to know that it is quite possible, and indeed much in the ordinary way of the world, for senile avarice and craft to set youth and bravery to work to win empire for it. He knows the pedigree of the child left on his hands, and nurses it to manhood with great care.

His pains are too well rewarded for his comfort. The boy Siegfried, having no god to instruct him in the art of unhappiness, inherits none of his father's ill luck, and all his father's hardihood. The fear against which Siegmund set his face like flint, and the woe which he wore down, are unknown to the son. The father was faithful and grateful: the son knows no law but his own humor; detests the ugly dwarf ho has nursed him; chafes furiously under his claims some return for his tender care; and is, in short, a totally unmoral person, a born anarchist, the ideal of Bakoonin, an anticipation of the "overman" of Nietzsche. He is enormously strong, full of life and fun, dangerous and destructive to what he dislikes, and affectionate to what he likes; so that it is fortunate that his likes and dislikes are sane and healthy. Altogether an inspiriting young forester, a son of the morning, in whom the heroic race has come out into the sunshine from the clouds of his grandfather's majestic entanglements with law, and the night of his father's tragic struggle with it.

The First Act

Mimmy's smithy is a cave, in which he hides from the light like the eyeless fish of the American caverns. Before the curtain rises the music already tells us that we are groping in darkness. When it does rise Mimmy is in difficulties. He is trying to make a sword for his nursling, who is now big enough to take the field against Fafnir. Mimmy can make mischievous swords; but it is not with dwarf made weapons that heroic man will hew the way of his own will through religions and governments and plutocracies and all the other devices of the kingdom of the fears of the unheroic. As fast as Mimmy makes swords, Siegfried Bakoonin smashes them, and then takes the poor old swordsmith by the scruff of the neck and chastises him wrathfully. The particular day on which the curtain rises begins with one of these trying domestic incidents. Mimmy has just done his best with a new sword of surpassing excellence. Siegfried returns home in rare spirits with a wild bear, to the extreme terror of the wretched dwarf. When the bear is dismissed, the new sword is produced. It is promptly smashed, as usual, with, also, the usual effects on the temper of Siegfried, who is quite boundless in his criticisms of the smith's boasted skill, and declares that he would smash the sword's maker too if he were not too disgusting to be handled.

Mimmy falls back on his stock defence: a string of maudlin reminders of the care with which he has nursed the little boy into manhood. Siegfried replies candidly that the strangest thing about all this care is that instead of making him grateful, it inspires him with a lively desire to wring the dwarf's neck. Only, he admits that he always comes back to his Mimmy, though he loathes him more than any living thing in the forest. On this admission the dwarf attempts to build a theory of filial instinct. He explains that he is Siegfried's father, and that this is why Siegfried cannot do without him. But Siegfried has learned from his forest companions, the birds and foxes and wolves, that mothers as well as fathers go to the making of children. Mimmy, on the desperate ground that man is neither bird nor fox, declares that he is Siegfried's father and mother both. He is promptly denounced as a filthy liar, because the birds and foxes are exactly like their parents, whereas Siegfried, having often watched his own image in the water, can testify that he is no more like Mimmy than a toad is like a trout. Then, to place the conversation on a plane of entire frankness, he throttles Mimmy until he is speechless. When the dwarf recovers, he is so daunted that he tells Siegfried the truth about his birth, and for testimony thereof produces the pieces of the sword that broke upon Wotan's spear. Siegfried instantly orders him to repair the sword on pain of an unmerciful thrashing, and rushes off into the forest, rejoicing in the discovery that he is no kin of Mimmy's, and need have no more to do with him when the sword is mended.

Poor Mimmy is now in a worse plight than ever; for he has long ago found that the sword utterly defies his skill: the steel will yield neither to his hammer nor to his furnace. Just then there walks into his cave a Wanderer, in a blue mantle, spear in hand, with one eye concealed by the brim of his wide hat. Mimmy, not by nature hospitable, tries to drive him away; but the Wanderer announces himself as a wise man, who can tell his host, in emergency, what it most concerns him to know. Mimmy, taking this offer in high dudgeon, because it implies that his visitor's wits are better than his own, offers to tell the wise one something that HE does not know: to wit, the way to the door. The imperturbable Wanderer's reply is to sit down and challenge the dwarf to a trial of wit. He wagers his head against Mimmy's that he will answer any three questions the dwarf can put to him.

Now here were Mimmy's opportunity, had he only the wit to ask what he wants to know, instead of pretending to know everything already. It is above all things needful to him at this moment to find out how that sword can be mended; and there has just dropped in upon him in his need the one person who can tell him. In such circumstances a wise man would hasten to show to his visitor his three deepest ignorances, and ask him to dispel them. The dwarf, being a crafty fool, desiring only to detect ignorance in his guest, asks him for information on the three points on which he is proudest of being thoroughly well instructed himself. His three questions are, Who dwell under the earth? Who dwell on the earth? and Who dwell in the cloudy heights above? The Wanderer, in reply, tells him of the dwarfs and of Alberic; of the earth, and the giants Fasolt and Fafnir; of the gods and of Wotan: himself, as Mimmy now recognizes with awe.

Next, it is Mimmy's turn to face three questions. What is that race, dearest to Wotan, against which Wotan has nevertheless done his worst? Mimmy can answer that: he knows the Volsungs, the race of heroes born of Wotan's infidelities to Fricka, and can tell the Wanderer the whole story of the twins and their son Siegfried. Wotan compliments him on his knowledge, and asks further with what sword Siegfried will slay Fafnir? Mimmy can answer that too: he has the whole history of the sword at his fingers' ends. Wotan hails him as the knowingest of the knowing, and then hurls at him the question he should himself have asked: Who will mend the sword? Mimmy, his head forfeited, confesses with loud lamentations that he cannot answer. The Wanderer reads him an appropriate little lecture on the folly of being too clever to ask what he wants to know, and informs him that a smith to whom fear is unknown will mend Nothung. To this smith he leaves the forfeited head of his host, and wanders off into the forest. Then Mimmy's nerves give way completely. He shakes like a man in delirium tremens, and has a horrible nightmare, in the supreme convulsion of which Siegfried, returning from the forest, presently finds him.

A curious and amusing conversation follows. Siegfried himself does not know fear, and is impatient to acquire it as an accomplishment. Mimmy is all fear: the world for him is a phantasmagoria of terrors. It is not that he is afraid of being eaten by bears in the forest, or of burning his fingers in the forge fire. A lively objection to being destroyed or maimed does not make a man a coward: on the contrary, it is the beginning of a brave man's wisdom. But in Mimmy, fear is not the effect of danger: it is natural quality of him which no security can allay. He is like many a poor newspaper editor, who dares not print the truth, however simple, even when it is obvious to himself and all his readers. Not that anything unpleasant would happen to him if he did—not, indeed that he could fail to become a distinguished and influential leader of opinion by fearlessly pursuing such a course, but solely because he lives in a world of imaginary terrors, rooted in a modest and gentlemanly mistrust of his own strength and worth, and consequently of the value of his opinion. Just so is Mimmy afraid of anything that can do him any good, especially of the light and the fresh air. He is also convinced that anybody who is not sufficiently steeped in fear to be constantly on his guard, must perish immediately on his first sally into the world. To preserve Siegfried for the enterprise to which he has destined him he makes a grotesque attempt to teach him fear. He appeals to his experience of the terrors of the forest, of its dark places, of its threatening noises its stealthy ambushes, its sinister flickering lights its heart—tightening ecstasies of dread.

All this has no other effect than to fill Siegfried with wonder and curiosity; for the forest is a place of delight for him. He is as eager to experience Mimmy's terrors as a schoolboy to feel what an electric shock is like. Then Mimmy has the happy idea of describing Fafnir to him as a likely person to give him an exemplary fright. Siegfried jumps at the idea, and, since Mimmy cannot mend the sword for him, proposes to set to work then and there to mend it for himself. Mimmy shakes his head, and bids him see now how his youthful laziness and frowardness have found him out—how he would not learn the smith's craft from Professor Mimmy, and therefore does not know how even to begin mending the sword. Siegfried Bakoonin's retort is simple and crushing. He points out that the net result of Mimmy's academic skill is that he can neither make a decent sword himself nor even set one to rights when it is damaged. Reckless of the remonstrances of the scandalized professor, he seizes a file, and in a few moments utterly destroys the fragments of the sword by rasping them into a heap of steel filings. Then he puts the filings into a crucible; buries it in the coals; and sets to at the bellows with the shouting exultation of the anarchist who destroys only to clear the ground for creation. When the steel is melted he runs it into a mould; and lo! a sword—blade in the rough. Mimmy, amazed at the success of this violation of all the rules of his craft, hails Siegfried as the mightiest of smiths, professing himself barely worthy to be his cook and scullion; and forthwith proceeds to poison some soup for him so that he may murder him safely when Fafnir is slain. Meanwhile Siegfned forges and tempers and hammers and rivets, uproariously singing the while as nonsensically as the Rhine maidens themselves. Finally he assails the anvil on which Mimmy's swords have been shattered, and cleaves it with a mighty stroke of the newly forged Nothung.

The Second Act

In the darkest hour before the dawn of that night, we find ourselves before the cave of Fafnir, and there we find Alberic, who can find nothing better to do with himself than to watch the haunt of the dragon, and eat his heart out in vain longing for the gold and the ring. The wretched Fafnir, once an honest giant, can only make himself terrible enough to keep his gold by remaining a venomous reptile. Why he should not become an honest giant again and clear out of his cavern, leaving the gold and the ring and the rest of it for anyone fool enough to take them at such a price, is the first question that would occur to anyone except a civilized man, who would be too accustomed to that sort of mania to be at all surprised at it.

To Alberic in the night comes the Wanderer, whom the dwarf, recognizing his despoiler of old, abuses as a shameless thief, taunting him with the helpless way in which all his boasted power is tied up with the laws and bargains recorded on the heft of his spear, which, says Alberic truly, would crumble like chaff in his hands if he dared use it for his own real ends. Wotan, having already had to kill his own son with it, knows that very well; but it troubles him no more; for he is now at last rising to abhorrence of his own artificial power, and looking to the coming hero, not for its consolidation but its destruction. When Alberic breaks out again with his still unquenched hope of one day destroying the gods and ruling the world through the ring, Wotan is no longer shocked. He tells Alberic that Brother Mime approaches with a hero whom Godhead can neither help nor hinder. Alberic may try his luck against him without disturbance from Valhalla. Perhaps, he suggests, if Alberic warns Fafnir, and offers to deal with the hero for him, Fafnir, may give him the ring. They accordingly wake up the dragon, who condescends to enter into bellowing conversation, but is proof against their proposition, strong in the magic of property. "I have and hold," he says: "leave me to sleep." Wotan, with a wise laugh, turns to Alberic. "That shot missed," he says: "no use abusing me for it. And now let me tell you one thing. All things happen according to their nature; and you can't alter them." And so he leaves him Alberic, raging with the sense that his old enemy has been laughing at him, and yet prophetically convinced that the last word will not be with the god, hides himself as the day breaks, and his brother approaches with Siegfried.

Mimmy makes a final attempt to frighten Siegfried by discoursing of the dragon's terrible jaws, poisonous breath, corrosive spittle, and deadly, stinging tail. Siegfried is not interested in the tail: he wants to know whether the dragon has a heart, being confident of his ability to stick Nothung into it if it exists. Reassured on this point, he drives Mimmy away, and stretches himself under the trees, listening to the morning chatter of the birds. One of them has a great deal to say to him; but he cannot understand it; and after vainly trying to carry on the conversation with a reed which he cuts, he takes to entertaining the bird with tunes on his horn, asking it to send him a loving mate such as all the other creatures of the forest have. His tunes wake up the dragon; and Siegfried makes merry over the grim mate the bird has sent him. Fafnir is highly scandalized by the irreverence of the young Bakoonin. He loses his temper; fights; and is forthwith slain, to his own great astonishment.

In such conflicts one learns to interpret the messages of Nature a little. When Siegfried, stung by the dragon's vitriolic blood, pops his finger into his mouth and tastes it, he understands what the bird is saying to him, and, instructed by it concerning the treasures within his reach, goes into the cave to secure the gold, the ring and the wishing cap. Then Mimmy returns, and is confronted by Alberic. The two quarrel furiously over the sharing of the booty they have not yet secured, until Siegfried comes from the cave with the ring and the helmet, not much impressed by the heap of gold, and disappointed because he has not yet learned to fear.

He has, however, learnt to read the thoughts of such a creature as poor Mimmy, who, intending to overwhelm him with flattery and fondness, only succeeds in making such a self–revelation of murderous envy that Siegfried smites him with Nothung and slays him, to the keen satisfaction of the hidden Alberic. Caring nothing for the gold, which he leaves to the care of the slain; disappointed in his fancy for learning fear; and longing for a mate, he casts himself wearily down, and again appeals to his friend the bird, who tells him of a woman sleeping on a mountain peak within a fortress of fire that only the fearless can penetrate. Siegfried is up in a moment with all the tumult of spring in his veins, and follows the flight of the bird as it pilots him to the fiery mountain.

The Third Act

To the root of the mountain comes also the Wanderer, now nearing his doom. He calls up the First Mother from the depths of the earth, and begs counsel from her. She bids him confer with the Norns (the Fates). But they are of no use to him: what he seeks is some foreknowledge of the way of the Will in its perpetual strife with these helpless Fates who can only spin the net of circumstance and environment round the feet of men. Why not, says Erda then, go to the daughter I bore you, and take counsel with her? He has to explain how he has cut himself off from her, and set the fires of Loki between the world and her counsel. In that case the First Mother cannot help him: such a separation is part of the bewilderment that is ever the first outcome of her eternal work of thrusting the life energy of the world to higher and higher organization. She can show him no way of escape from the destruction he foresees. Then from the innermost of him breaks the confession that he rejoices in his doom, and now himself exults in passing away with all his ordinances and alliances, with the spear–sceptre which he has only wielded on condition of slaying his dearest children with it, with the kingdom, the power and the glory which will never again boast themselves as "world without end." And so he dismisses Erda to her sleep in the heart of the earth as the forest bird draws near, piloting the slain son's son to his goal.

Now it is an excellent thing to triumph in the victory of the new order and the passing away of the old; but if you happen to be part of the old order yourself, you must none the less fight for your life. It seems hardly possible that the British army at the battle of Waterloo did not include at least one Englishman intelligent enough to hope, for the sake of his country and humanity, that Napoleon might defeat the allied sovereigns; but such an Englishman would kill a French cuirassier rather than be killed by him just as energetically as the silliest soldier, ever encouraged by people who ought to know better, to call his ignorance, ferocity and folly, patriotism and duty. Outworn life may have become mere error; but it still claims the right to die a natural death, and will raise its hand against the millennium itself in self–defence if it tries to come by the short cut of murder. Wotan finds this out when he comes face to face with Siegfried, who is brought to a standstill at the foot of the mountain by the disappearance of the bird. Meeting the Wanderer there, he asks him the way to the mountain where a woman sleeps surrounded by fire. The Wanderer questions him, and extracts his story from him, breaking into fatherly delight when Siegfried, describing the mending of the sword remarks, that all he knew about the business was that the broken bits of Nothung would be of no use to him unless he made a new sword out of them right over again from the beginning. But the Wanderer's interest is by no means reciprocated by Siegfried. His majesty and elderly dignity are thrown away on the young anarchist, who, unwilling to waste time talking, bluntly bids him either show him the way to the mountain, or else "shut his muzzle." Wotan is a little hurt. "Patience, my lad," he says: "if you were an old man I should treat you with respect." "That would be a precious notion," says Siegfried. "All my life long I was bothered and hampered by an old man until I swept him out of my way. I will sweep you in the same fashion if you don't let me pass. Why do you wear such a big hat; and what has happened to one of your eyes? Was it knocked out by somebody whose way you obstructed?" To which Wotan replies allegorically that the eye that is gone—the eye that his marriage with Fricka cost him—is now looking at him out of Siegfried's head. At this, Siegfried gives up the Wanderer as a lunatic, and renews his threats of personal violence. Then Wotan throws off the mask of the Wanderer; uplifts the world–governing spear; and puts forth all his divine awe and grandeur as the guardian of the mountain, round the crest of which the fires of Loki now break into a red background for the majesty of the god. But all this is lost on Siegfried Bakoonin. "Aha!" he cries, as the spear is levelled against his breast: "I have found my father's foe"; and the spear falls in two pieces under the stroke of Nothung. "Up then," says Wotan: "I cannot withhold you," and disappears forever from the eye of man. The fires roll down the mountain; but Siegfried goes at them as exultantly as he went at the forging of the sword or the heart of the dragon, and shoulders his way through them, joyously sounding his horn to the accompaniment of their crackling and seething. And never a hair of his head is singed. Those frightful flames which have scared mankind for centuries from the Truth, have not heat enough in them to make a child shut its eyes. They are mere phantasmagoria, highly creditable to Loki's imaginative stage–management; but nothing ever has perished or will perish eternally in them except the Churches which nave been so poor and faithless as to trade for their power on the lies of a romancer.

BACK TO OPERA AGAIN

And now, O Nibelungen Spectator, pluck up; for all allegories come to an end somewhere; and the hour of your release from these explanations is at hand. The rest of what you are going to see is opera, and nothing but opera. Before many bars have been played, Siegfried and the wakened Brynhild, newly become tenor and soprano, will sing a concerted cadenza; plunge on from that to a magnificent love duet; and end with a precipitous allegro a capella, driven headlong to its end by the impetuous semiquaver triplets of the famous finales to the first act of Don Giovanni or the coda to the Leonore overture, with a specifically contrapuntal theme, points d'orgue, and a high C for the soprano all complete.

What is more, the work which follows, entitled Night Falls On The Gods, is a thorough grand opera. In it you shall see what you have so far missed, the opera chorus in full parade on the stage, not presuming to interfere with the prima donna as she sings her death song over the footlights. Nay, that chorus will have its own chance when it first appears, with a good roaring strain in C major, not, after all, so very different from, or at all less absurd than the choruses of courtiers in La Favorita or "Per te immenso giubilo" in Lucia. The harmony is no doubt a little developed, Wagner augmenting his fifths with a G sharp where Donizetti would have put his fingers in his ears and screamed for G natural. But it is an opera chorus all the same; and along with it we have theatrical grandiosities that recall Meyerbeer and Verdi: pezzi d'insieme for all the principals in a row, vengeful conjurations for trios of them, romantic death song for the tenor: in short, all manner of operatic conventions.

Now it is probable that some of us will have been so talked by the more superstitious Bayreuth pilgrims into regarding Die Gotterdammerung as the mighty climax to a mighty epic, more Wagnerian than all the other three sections put together, as not to dare notice this startling atavism, especially if we find the trio–conjurations more exhilarating than the metaphysical discourses of Wotan in the three true music dramas of The Ring. There is, however, no real atavism involved. Die Gotterdammerung, though the last of The Ring dramas in order of performance, was the first in order of conception and was indeed the root from which all the others sprang.

The history of the matter is as follows. All Wagner's works prior to The Ring are operas. The last of them, Lohengrin, is perhaps the best known of modern operas. As performed in its entirety at Bayreuth, it is even more operatic than it appears at Covent Garden, because it happens that its most old–fashioned features, notably some of the big set concerted pieces for principals and chorus (pezzi d'insieme as I have called them above), are harder to perform than the more modern and characteristically Wagnerian sections, and for that reason were cut out in preparing the abbreviated fashionable version. Thus Lohengrin came upon the ordinary operatic stage as a more advanced departure from current operatic models than its composer had made it. Still, it is unmistakably an opera, with chorus, concerted pieces, grand finales, and a heroine who, if she does not sing florid variations with flute obbligato, is none the less a very perceptible prima donna. In everything but musical technique the change from Lohengrin to The Rhine Gold is quite revolutionary.

The explanation is that Night Falls On The Gods came in between them, although its music was not finished until twenty years after that of The Rhine Gold, and thus belongs to a later and more masterful phase of Wagner's harmonic style. It first came into

Wagner's head as an opera to be entitled Siegfied's Death, founded on the old Niblung Sagas, which offered to Wagner the same material for an effective theatrical tragedy as they did to Ibsen. Ibsen's Vikings in Helgeland is, in kind, what Siegfied's Death was originally intended to be: that is, a heroic piece for the theatre, without the metaphysical or allegorical complications of The Ring. Indeed, the ultimate catastrophe of the Saga cannot by any perversion of ingenuity be adapted to the perfectly clear allegorical design of The Rhine Gold, The Valkyries, and Siegfried.

SIEGFRIED AS PROTESTANT

The philosophically fertile element in the original project of Siegfried's Death was the conception of Siegfried himself as a type of the healthy man raised to perfect confidence in his own impulses by an intense and joyous vitality which is above fear, sickliness of conscience, malice, and the makeshifts and moral crutches of law and order which accompany them. Such a character appears extraordinarily fascinating and exhilarating to our guilty and conscience–ridden generations, however little they may understand him. The world has always delighted in the man who is delivered from conscience. From Punch and Don Juan down to Robert Macaire, Jeremy Diddler and the pantomime clown, he has always drawn large audiences; but hitherto he has been decorously given to the devil at the end. Indeed eternal punishment is sometimes deemed too high a compliment to his nature. When the late Lord Lytton, in his Strange Story, introduced a character personifying the joyousness of intense vitality, he felt bound to deny him the immortal soul which was at that time conceded even to the humblest characters in fiction, and to accept mischievousness, cruelty, and utter incapacity for sympathy as the inevitable consequence of his magnificent bodily and mental health.

In short, though men felt all the charm of abounding life and abandonment to its impulses, they dared not, in their deep self–mistrust, conceive it otherwise than as a force making for evil—one which must lead to universal ruin unless checked and literally mortified by selfrenunciation in obedience to superhuman guidance, or at least to some reasoned system of morals. When it became apparent to the cleverest of them that no such superhuman guidance existed, and that their secularist systems had all the fictitiousness of "revelation" without its poetry, there was no escaping the conclusion that all the good that man had done must be put down to his arbitrary will as well as all the evil he had done; and it was also obvious that if progress were a reality, his beneficent impulses must be gaining on his destructive ones. It was under the influence of these ideas that we began to hear about the joy of life where we had formerly heard about the grace of God or the Age of Reason, and that the boldest spirits began to raise the question whether churches and laws and the like were not doing a great deal more harm than good by their action in limiting the freedom of the human will. Four hundred years ago, when belief in God and in revelation was general throughout Europe, a similar wave of thought led the strongest-hearted peoples to affirm that every man's private judgment was a more trustworthy interpreter of God and revelation than the Church. This was called Protestantism; and though the Protestants were not strong enough for their creed, and soon set up a Church of their own, yet the movement, on the whole, has justified the direction it took. Nowadays the supernatural element in Protestantism has perished; and if every man's private judgment is still to be justified as the most trustworthy interpreter of the will of Humanity (which is not a more extreme proposition than the old one about the will of God) Protestantism must take a fresh step in advance, and become Anarchism. Which it has accordingly done, Anarchism being one of the notable new creeds of the eighteenth and nineteenth centuries.

The weak place which experience finds out in the Anarchist theory is its reliance on the progress already achieved by "Man." There is no such thing as Man in the world: what we have to deal with is a multitude of men, some of them great rascals, some of them greet statesmen, others both, with a vast majority capable of managing their personal affairs, but not of comprehending social organization, or grappling with the problems created by their association in enormous numbers. If "Man" means this majority, then "Man" has made no progress: he has, on the contrary, resisted it. He will not even pay the cost of existing institutions: the requisite money has to be filched from him by "indirect taxation." Such people, like Wagner's giants; must be governed by laws; and their assent to such government must be secured by deliberately filling them with prejudices and practicing on their imaginations by pageantry and artificial eminences and dignities. The government is of course established by the few who are capable of government, though its mechanism once complete, it may be, and generally is, carried on unintelligently by people who are incapable of it the capable people repairing it from time to time when it gets too far behind the continuous advance or decay of civilization. All these capable people are thus in the position of Wotan, forced to maintain as sacred, and themselves submit to, laws which they privately know to be obsolescent makeshifts, and to affect the deepest veneration for creeds and ideals which they ridicule among themselves with cynical scepticism. No individual Siegfried can rescue them from this bondage and hypocrisy; in fact, the individual Siegfried has come often enough, only to find himself confronted with the alternative of governing those who are not Siegfrieds or risking destruction at their hands. And this dilemma will persist until Wotan's inspiration comes to our governors, and they see that their business is not the devising of laws and institutions to prop up the weaknesses of mobs and secure the survival of the unfittest, but the breeding of men whose wills and intelligences may be depended on to produce spontaneously the social wellbeing our clumsy laws now aim at and miss. The majority of men at present in Europe have no business to be alive; and no serious progress will be made until we address ourselves earnestly and scientifically to the task of producing trustworthy human materialfor society. In short, it is necessary to breed a race of men in whom the life–giving impulses predominate, before the New Protestantism becomes politically practicable.*

*The necessity for breeding the governing class from a selected stock has always been recognized by Aristocrats, however erroneous their methods of selection. We have changed our system from Aristocracy to Democracy without considering that we were at the same time changing, as regards our governing class, from Selection to Promiscuity. Those who have taken a practical part in modern politics best know how farcical the result is.

The most inevitable dramatic conception, then, of the nineteenth century, is that of a perfectly naive hero upsetting religion, law and order in all directions, and establishing in their place the unfettered action of Humanity doing exactly what it likes, and producing order instead of confusion thereby because it likes to do what is necessary for the good of the race. This conception, already incipient in Adam Smith's Wealth of Nations, was certain at last to reach some great artist, and be embodied by him in a masterpiece. It was also certain that if that master happened to be a German, he should take delight in describing his hero as the Freewiller of Necessity, thereby beyond measure exasperating Englishmen with a congenital incapacity for metaphysics.

PANACEA QUACKERY, OTHERWISE IDEALISM

Unfortunately, human enlightenment does not progress by nicer and nicer adjustments, but by violent corrective reactions which invariably send us clean over our saddle and would bring us to the ground on the other side if the next reaction did not send us back again with equally excessive zeal. Ecclesiasticism and Constitutionalism send us one way, Protestantism and Anarchism the other; Order rescues us from confusion and lands us in Tyranny; Liberty then saves the situation and is presently found to be as great a nuisance as Despotism. A scientifically balanced application of these forces, theoretically possible, is practically incompatible with human passion. Besides, we have the same weakness in morals as in medicine: we cannot be cured of running after panaceas, or, as they are called in the sphere of morals, ideals. One generation sets up duty, renunciation, self–sacrifice as a panacea. The next generation, especially the women, wake up at the age of forty or thereabouts to the fact that their lives have been wasted in the worship of this ideal, and, what is still more aggravating, that the elders who imposed it on them did so in a fit of satiety with their own experiments in the other direction. Then that defrauded generation foams at the mouth at the very mention of duty, and sets up the alternative panacea of love, their deprivation of which seems to them to have been the most cruel and mischievous feature of their slavery to duty. It is useless to warn them that this reaction, if prescribed as a panacea, will prove as great a failure as all the other reactions have done; for they do not recognize its identity with any reaction that ever occurred before. Take for instance the hackneyed historic example of the austerity of the Commonwealth being followed by the licence of the Restoration. You cannot persuade any moral enthusiast to accept this as a pure oscillation from action to reaction. If he is a Puritan he looks upon the Restoration as a national disaster: if he is an artist he regards it as the salvation of the country from gloom, devil worship and starvation of the affections. The Puritan is ready to try the Commonwealth again with a few modern improvements: the Amateur is equally ready to try the Restoration with modern enlightenments. And so for the present we must be content to proceed by reactions, hoping that each will establish some permanently practical and beneficial reform or moral habit that will survive the correction of its excesses by the next reaction.

DRAMATIC ORIGIN OF WOTAN

We can now see how a single drama in which Wotan does not appear, and of which Siegfried is the hero, expanded itself into a great fourfold drama of which Wotan is the hero. You cannot dramatize a reaction by personifying the reacting force only, any more than Archimedes could lift the world without a fulcrum for his lever. You must also personify the established power against which the new force is reacting; and in the conflict between them you get your drama, conflict being the essential ingredient in all drama. Siegfried, as the hero of Die Gotterdammerung, is only the primo tenore robusto of an opera book, deferring his death, after he has been stabbed in the last act, to sing rapturous love strains to the heroine exactly like Edgardo in Donizetti's Lucia. In order to make him intelligible in the wider significance which his joyous, fearless, conscienceless heroism soon assumed in Wagner's imagination, it was necessary to provide him with a much vaster dramatic antagonist than the operatic villain Hagen. Hence Wagner had to create Wotan as the anvil for Siegfried's hammer; and since there was no room for Wotan in the original opera book, Wagner had to work back to a preliminary drama reaching primarily to the very beginnings of human society. And since, on this world—embracing scale, it was clear that Siegfried must come into conflict with many baser and stupider forces than those lofty ones of supernatural religion and political constitutionalism typified by Wotan and his wife Fricka, these minor antagonists had to be dramatized also in the persons of Alberic, Mime, Fafnir, Loki, and the rest. None of these appear in Night Falls On The Gods save Alberic, whose weird dream—colloquy with Hagen, effective as it is, is as purely theatrical as the scene of the Ghost in Hamlet, or the statue in Don Giovanni. Cut the conference of the Norns and the visit of Valtrauta to Brynhild out of Night Falls On The Gods, and the drama remains coherent and complete without them. Retain them, and the play becomes connected by conversational references with the three music dramas; but the connection establishes no philosophic coherence, no real identity between the operatic Brynhild of the Gibichung episode (presently to be related) and the daughter of Wotan and the First Mother.

THE LOVE PANACEA

We shall now find that at the point where The Ring changes from music drama into opera, it also ceases to be philosophic, and becomes didactic. The philosophic part is a dramatic symbol of the world as Wagner observed it. In the didactic part the philosophy degenerates into the prescription of a romantic nostrum for all human ills. Wagner, only mortal after all, succumbed to the panacea mania when his philosophy was exhausted, like any of the rest of us.

The panacea is by no means an original one. Wagner was anticipated in the year 1819 by a young country gentleman from Sussex named Shelley, in a work of extraordinary artistic power and splendor. Prometheus Unbound is an English attempt at a Ring; and when it is taken into account that the author was only 27 whereas Wagner was 40 when he completed the poem of The Ring, our vulgar patriotism may find an envious satisfaction in insisting upon the comparison. Both works set forth the same conflict between humanity and its gods and governments, issuing in the redemption of man from their tyranny by the growth of his will into perfect strength and self–confidence; and both finish by a lapse into panacea–mongering didacticism by the holding up of Love as the remedy for all evils and the solvent of all social difficulties.

The differences between Prometheus Unbound and The Ring are as interesting as the likenesses. Shelley, caught in the pugnacity of his youth and the first impetuosity of his prodigious artistic power by the first fierce attack of the New Reformation, gave no quarter to the antagonist of his hero. His Wotan, whom he calls Jupiter, is the almighty fiend into whom the Englishman's God had degenerated during two centuries of ignorant Bible worship and shameless commercialism. He is Alberic, Fafnir Loki and the ambitious side of Wotan all rolled into one melodramatic demon who is finally torn from his throne and hurled shrieking into the abyss by a spirit representing that conception of Eternal Law which has been replaced since by the conception of Evolution. Wagner, an older, more experienced man than the Shelley of 1819, understood Wotan and pardoned him, separating him tenderly from all the compromising alliances to which Shelley fiercely held him; making the truth and heroism which overthrow him the children of his inmost heart; and representing him as finally acquiescing in and working for his own supersession and annihilation. Shelley, in his later works, is seen progressing towards the same tolerance, justice, and humility of spirit, as he advanced towards the middle age he never reached. But there is no progress from Shelley to Wagner as regards the panacea, except that in Wagner there is a certain shadow of night and death come on it: nay, even a clear opinion that the supreme good of love is that it so completely satisfies the desire for life, that after it the Will to Live ceases to trouble us, and we are at last content to achieve the highest happiness of death.

This reduction of the panacea to absurdity was not forced upon Shelley, because the love which acts as a universal solvent in his Prometheus Unbound is a sentiment of affectionate benevolence which has nothing to do with sexual passion. It might, and in fact does exist in the absence of any sexual interest whatever. The words mercy and kindness connote it less ambiguously than the word love. But Wagner sought always for some point of contact between his ideas and the physical senses, so that people might not only think or imagine them in the eighteenth century fashion, but see them on the stage, hear them from the orchestra, and feel them through the infection of passionate emotion. Dr. Johnson kicking the stone to confute Berkeley is not more bent on common–sense concreteness than Wagner: on all occasions he insists on the need for sensuous apprehension to give reality to abstract comprehension, maintaining, in fact, that reality has no other meaning. Now he could apply this process to poetic love only by following it back to its alleged origin in sexual passion, the emotional phenomena of which he has expressed in music with a frankness and forcible naturalism which would possibly have scandalized Shelley. The love duet in the first act of The Valkyries is brought to a point at which the conventions of our society demand the precipitate fall of the curtain; whilst the prelude to Tristan and Isolde is such an astonishingly intense and faithful translation into music of the emotions which accompany the union of a pair of lovers, that it is questionable whether the great popularity of this piece at our orchestral concerts really means that our audiences are entirely catholic in their respect for life in all itits beneficently creative functions, or whether they simply enjoy the music without understanding it.

But however offensive and inhuman may be the superstition which brands such exaltations of natural passion as shameful and indecorous, there is at least as much common sense in disparaging love as in setting it up as a panacea. Even the mercy and lovingkindness of Shelley do not hold good as a universal law of conduct: Shelley himself makes extremely short work of Jupiter, just as Siegfried does of Fafnir, Mime, and Wotan; and the fact that Prometheus is saved from doing the destructive part of his work by the intervention of that very nebulous personification of Eternity called Demogorgon, does not in the least save the situation, because, flatly, there is no such person as Demogorgon, and if Prometheus does not pull down Jupiter himself, no one else will. It would be exasperating, if it were not so funny, to see these poets leading their heroes through blood and destruction to the conclusion that, as Browning's David puts it (David of all people!), "All's Love; yet all's Law."

Certainly it is clear enough that such love as that implied by Siegfried's first taste of fear as he cuts through the mailed coat of the sleeping figure on the mountain, and discovers that it is a woman; by her fierce revolt against being touched by him when his terror gives way to ardor; by his manly transports of victory; and by the womanly mixture of rapture and horror with which she abandons herself to the passion which has seized on them both, is an experience which it is much better, like the vast majority of us, never to have passed through, than to allow it to play more than a recreative holiday part in our lives. It did not play a very large part in Wagner's own laborious life, and does not occupy more than two scenes of The Ring. Tristan and Isolde, wholly devoted to it, is a poem of destruction and death. The Mastersingers, a work full of health, fun and happiness, contains not a single bar of love music that can be described as passionate: the hero of it

47

is a widower who cobbles shoes, writes verses, and contents himself with looking on at the sweetheartings of his customers. Parsifal makes an end of it altogether. The truth is that the love panacea in Night Falls On The Gods and in the last act of Siegfried is a survival of the first crude operatic conception of the story, modified by an anticipation of Wagner's later, though not latest, conception of love as the fulfiller of our Will to Live and consequently our reconciler to night and death.

NOT LOVE, BUT LIFE

The only faith which any reasonable disciple can gain from The Ring is not in love, but in life itself as a tireless power which is continually driving onward and upward—not, please observe, being beckoned or drawn by Das Ewig Weibliche or any other external sentimentality, but growing–from within, by its own inexplicable energy, into ever higher and higher forms of organization, the strengths and the needs of which are continually superseding the institutions which were made to fit our former requirements. When your Bakoonins call out for the demolition of all these venerable institutions, there is no need to fly into a panic and lock them up in prison whilst your parliament is bit by bit doing exactly what they advised you to do. When your Siegfrieds melt down the old weapons into new ones, and with disrespectful words chop in twain the antiquated constable's staves in the hands of their elders, the end of the world is no nearer than it was before. If human nature, which is the highest organization of life reached on this planet, is really degenerating, then human society will decay; and no panic–begotten penal measures can possibly save it: we must, like Prometheus, set to work to make new men instead of vainly torturing old ones. On the other hand, if the energy of life is still carrying human nature to higher and higher levels, then the more young people shock their elders and deride and discard their pet institutions the better for the hopes of the world, since the apparent growth of anarchy is only the measure of the rate of improvement. History, as far as we are capable of history (which is not saying much as yet), shows that all changes from crudity of social organization to complexity, and from mechanical agencies in government to living ones, seem anarchic at first sight. No doubt it is natural to a snail to think that any evolution which threatens to do away with shells will result in general death from exposure. Nevertheless, the most elaborately housed beings today are born not only without houses on their backs but without even fur or feathers to clothe them.

ANARCHISM NO PANACEA

One word of warning to those who may find themselves attracted by Siegfried's Anarchism, or, if they prefer a term with more respectable associations, his neo–Protestantism. Anarchism, as a panacea, is just as hopeless as any other panacea, and will still be so even if we breed a race of perfectly benevolent men. It is true that in the sphere of thought, Anarchism is an inevitable condition of progressive evolution. A nation without Freethinkers—that is, without intellectual Anarchists—will share the fate of China. It is also true that our criminal law, based on a conception of crime and punishment which is nothing but our vindictiveness and cruelty in a virtuous disguise, is an unmitigated and abominable nuisance, bound to be beaten out of us finally by the mere weight of our experience of its evil and uselessness. But it will not be replaced by anarchy. Applied to the industrial or political machinery of modern society, anarchy must always reduce itself speedily to absurdity. Even the modified form of anarchy on which modern civilization is based: that is, the abandonment of industry, in the name of individual liberty, to the upshot of competition for personal gain between private capitalists, is a disastrous failure, and is, by the mere necessities of the case, giving way to ordered Socialism. For the economic rationale of this, I must refer disciples of Siegfried to a tract from my hand published by the Fabian Society and entitled The Impossibilities of Anarchism, which explains why, owing to the physical constitution of our globe, society cannot effectively organize the production of its food, clothes and housing, nor distribute them fairly and economically on any anarchic plan: nay, that without concerting our social action to a much higher degree than we do at present we can never get rid of the wasteful and iniquitous welter of a little riches and a deal of poverty which current political humbug calls our prosperity and civilization. Liberty is an excellent thing; but it cannot begin until society has paid its daily debt to Nature by first earning its living. There is no liberty before that except the liberty to live at somebody else's expense, a liberty much sought after nowadays, since it is the criterion of gentility, but not wholesome from the point of view of the common weal.

SIEGFRIED CONCLUDED

In returning now to the adventures of Siegfried there is little more to be described except the finale of an opera. Siegfried, having passed unharmed through the fire, wakes Brynhild and goes through all the fancies and ecstasies of love at first sight in a duet which ends with an apostrophe to "leuchtende Liebe, lachender Tod!", which has been romantically translated into "Love that illumines, laughing at Death," whereas it really identifies enlightening love and laughing death as involving each other so closely as to be usually one and the same thing.

NIGHT FALLS ON THE GODS

PROLOGUE

Die Gottrerdammerung begins with an elaborate prologue. The three Norns sit in the night on Brynhild's mountain top spinning their thread of destiny, and telling the story of Wotan's sacrifice of his eye, and of his breaking off a bough from the World Ash to make a heft for his spear, also how the tree withered after suffering that violence. They have also some fresher news to discuss. Wotan, on the breaking of his spear by Siegfried, has called all his heroes to cut down the withered World Ash and stack its faggots in a mighty pyre about Valhalla. Then, with his broken spear in his hand, he has seated himself in state in the great hall, with the Gods and Heroes assembled about him as if in council, solemnly waiting for the end. All this belongs to the old legendary materials with which Wagner began The Ring.

The tale is broken by the thread snapping in the hands of the third Norn; for the hour has arrived when man has taken his destiny in his own hands to shape it for himself, and no longer bows to circumstance, environment, necessity (which he now freely wills), and all the rest of the inevitables. So the Norns recognize that the world has no further use for them, and sink into the earth to return to the First Mother. Then the day dawns; and Siegfried and Brynhild come, and have another duet. He gives her his ring; and she gives him her horse. Away then he goes in search of more adventures; and she watches him from her crag until he disappears. The curtain falls; but we can still hear the trolling of his horn, and the merry clatter of his horse's shoes trotting gaily down the valley. The sound is lost in the grander rhythm of the Rhine as he reaches its banks. We hear again an echo of the lament of the Rhine maidens for the ravished gold; and then, finally, a new strain, which does not surge like the mighty flood of the river, but has an unmistakable tramp of hardy men and a strong land flavor about it. And on this the opera curtain at last goes up—for please remember that all that has gone before is only the overture.

The First Act

We now understand the new tramping strain. We are in the Rhineside hall of the

Gibichungs, in the resence of King Gunther, his sister Gutrune, and unther's grim half brother Hagen, the villain of the piece. Gunther is a fool, and has for Hagen's intelligence the respect a fool always has for the brains of a scoundrel. Feebly fishing for compliments, he appeals to Hagen to pronounce him a fine fellow and a glory to the race of Gibich. Hagen declares that it is impossible to contemplate him without envy, but thinks it a pity that he has not yet found a wife glorious enough for him. Gunther doubts whether so extraordinary a person can possibly exist. Hagen then tells him of Brynhild and her rampart of fire; also of Siegfried. Gunther takes this rather in bad part, since not only is he afraid of the fire, but Siegfried, according to Hagen, is not, and will therefore achieve this desirable match himself. But Hagen points out that since Siegfried is riding about in quest of adventures, he will certainly pay an early visit to the renowned chief of the Gibichungs. They can then give him a philtre which will make him fall in love with Gutrune and forget every other woman he has yet seen.

Gunther is transported with admiration of Hagen's cunning when he takes in this plan; and he has hardly assented to it when Siegfried, with operatic opportuneness, drops in just as Hagen expected, and is duly drugged into the heartiest love for Gutrune and total oblivion of Brynhild and his own past. When Gunther declares his longing for the bride who lies inaccessible within a palisade of flame, Siegfried at once offers to undertake the adventure for him. Hagen then explains to both of them that Siegfried can, after braving the fire, appear to Brynhild in the semblance of Gunther through the magic of the wishing cap (or Tarnhelm, as it is called throughout The Ring), the use of which Siegfried now learns for the first time. It is of course part of the bargain that Gunther shall give his sister to Siegfried in marriage. On that they swear blood–brotherhood; and at this opportunity the old operatic leaven breaks out amusingly in Wagner. With tremendous exordium of brass, the tenor and baritone go at it with a will, showing off the power of their voices, following each other in canonic imitation, singing together in thirds and sixths, and finishing with a lurid unison, quite in the manner of Ruy Gomez and Ernani, or Othello and Iago. Then without further ado Siegfried departs on his expedition, taking Gunther with him to the foot of the mountain, and leaving Hagen to guard the hall and sing a very fine solo which has often figured in the programs of the Richter concerts, explaining that his interest in the affair is that Siegfried will bring back the Ring, and that he, Hagen, will presently contrive to possess himself of that Ring and become Plutonic master of the world.

And now it will be asked how does Hagen know all about the Plutonic empire; and why was he able to tell Gunther about Brynhild and Siegfried, and to explain to Siegfried the trick of the Tarnhelm. The explanation is that though Hagen's mother was the mother of Gunther, his father was not the illustrious Gibich, but no less a person than our old friend Alberic, who, like Wotan, has begotten a son to do for him what he cannot do for himself.

In the above incidents, those gentle moralizers who find the serious philosophy of the music dramas too terrifying for them, may allegorize pleasingly on the philtre as the maddening chalice of passion which, once tasted, causes the respectable man to forget his lawfully wedded wife and plunge into adventures which eventually lead him headlong to destruction.

We now come upon a last relic of the tragedy of Wotan. Returning to Brynhild's mountain, we find her visited by her sister Valkyrie Valtrauta, who has witnessed Wotan's solemn preparations with terror. She repeats to Brynhild the account already given by the Norns. Clinging in anguish to Wotan's knees, she has heard him mutter that were the ring returned to the daughters of the deep Rhine, both Gods and world would be redeemed from that stage curse off Alberic's in The Rhine Gold. On this she has rushed on her warhorse through the air to beg Brynhild to give the Rhine back its ring. But this is asking Woman to give up love for the sake of Church and State. She declares that she will see them both perish first; and Valtrauta returns to Valhalla in despair. Whilst Brynhild is watching the course of the black thundercloud that marks her sister's flight, the fires of Loki again flame high round the mountain; and the horn of Siegfried is heard as he makes his way through them. But the man who now appears wears the Tarnhelm: his voice is a strange voice: his figure is the unknown one of the king of the Gibichungs. He tears the ring from her finger, and, claiming her as his wife, drives her into the cave without pity for her agony of horror, and sets Nothung between them in token of his loyalty to the friend he is impersonating. No explanation of this highway robbery of the ring is offered. Clearly, this Siegfried is not the Siegfried of the previous drama.

The Second Act

In the second act we return to the hall of Gibich, where Hagen, in the last hours of that night, still sits, his spear in his hand, and his shield beside him. At his knees crouches a dwarfish spectre, his father Alberic, still full of his old grievances against Wotan, and urging his son in his dreams to win back the ring for him. This Hagen swears to do; and as the apparition of his father vanishes, the sun rises and Siegfried suddenly comes from the river bank tucking into his belt the Tarnhelm, which has transported hi from the mountain like the enchanted carpet of the Arabian tales. He describes his adventures to Gutrune until Gunther's boat is seen approaching, when Hagen seizes a cowhorn and calls the tribesmen to welcome their chief and his bride. It is most exhilarating, this colloquy with the startled and hastily armed clan, ending with a thundering chorus, the drums marking the time with mighty pulses from dominant to tonic, much as Rossini would have made them do if he had been a pupil of Beethoven's.

A terrible scene follows. Gunther leads his captive bride straight into the presence of Siegfried, whom she claims as her husband by the ring, which she is astomshed to see on his finger: Gunther, as she supposes, having torn it from her the night before. Turning on Gunther, she says "Since you took that ring from me, and married me with it, tell him of your right to it; and make him give it back to you." Gunther stammers, "The ring! I gave him no ring—er—do you know him?" The rejoinder is obvious. "Then where are you hiding the ring that you had from me?" Gunther's confusion enlightens her; and she calls Siegfried trickster and thief to his face. In vain he declares that he got the ring from no woman, but from a dragon whom he slew; for he is manifestly puzzled; and she, seizing her opportunity, accuses him before the clan of having played Gunther false with her.

Hereupon we have another grandiose operatic oath, Siegfried attesting his innocence on Hagen's spear, and Brynhild rushing to the footlights and thrusting him aside to attest his guilt, whilst the clansmen call upon their gods to send down lightnings and silence the perjured. The gods do not respond; and Siegfried, after whispering to Gunther that the Tarnhelm seems to have been only half effectual after all, laughs his way out of the general embarrassment and goes off merrily to prepare for his wedding, with his arm round Gutrune's waist, followed by the clan. Gunther, Hagen and Brynhild are left together to plot operatic vengeance. Brynhild, it appears, has enchanted Siegfried in such a fashion that no weapon can hurt him. She has, however, omitted to protect his back, since it is impossible that he should ever turn that to a foe. They agree accordingly that on the morrow a great hunt shall take place, at which Hagen shall thrust his spear into the hero's vulnerable back. The blame is to be laid on the tusk of a wild boar. Gunther, being a fool, is remorseful about his oath of blood—brotherhood and about his sister's bereavement, without having the strength of mind to prevent the murder. The three burst into a herculean trio, similar in conception to that of the three conspirators in Un Ballo in Maschera; and the act concludes with a joyous strain heralding the appearance of

SiegEried's wedding procession, with strewing of flowers, sacrificing to the gods, and carrying bride and bridegroom in triumph.

It will be seen that in this act we have lost all connection with the earlier drama. Brynhild is not only not the Brynhild of The Valkyries, she is the Hiordis of Ibsen, a majestically savage woman, in whom jealousy and revenge are intensified to heroic proportions. That is the inevitable theatrical treatment of the murderous heroine of the Saga. Ibsen's aim in The Vikings was purely theatrical, and not, as in his later dramas, also philosophically symbolic. Wagner's aim in Siegfried's Death was equally theatrical, and not, as it afterwards became in the dramas of which Siegfried s antagonist Wotan is the hero, likewise philosophically symbolic. The two master–dramatists therefore produce practically the same version of Brynhild. Thus on the second evening of The Ring we see Brynhild in the character of the truth–divining instinct in religion, cast into an enchanted slumber and surrounded by the fires of hell lest she should overthrow a Church corrupted by its alliance with government. On the fourth evening, we find her swearing a malicious lie to gratify her personal jealousy, and then plotting a treacherous murder with a fool and a scoundrel. In the original draft of Siegfried's Death, the incongruity is carried still further by the conclusion, at which the dead Brynhild, restored to her godhead by Wotan, and again a Valkyrie, carries the slain Siegfried to Valhalla to live there happily ever after with its pious heroes.

As to Siegfried himself, he talks of women, both in this second act and the next, with the air of a man of the world. "Their tantrums," he says, "are soon over." Such speeches do not belong to the novice of the preceding drama, but to the original Siegfried's Tod, with its leading characters sketched on the ordinary romantic lines from the old Sagas, and not yet reminted as the original creations of Wagner's genius whose acquaintance we have made on the two previous evenings. The very title "Siegfried's Death" survives as a strong theatrical point in the following passage. Gunther, in his rage and despair, cries, "Save me, Hagen: save my honor and thy mother's who bore us both." "Nothing can save thee," replies Hagen: "neither brain nor hand, but SIEGFRIED'S DEATH." And Gunther echoes with a shudder, "SIEGFRIED'S DEATH!"

A WAGNERIAN NEWSPAPER CONTROVERSY

The devotion which Wagner's work inspires has been illustrated lately in a public correspondence on this very point. A writer in The Daily Telegraph having commented on the falsehood uttered by Brynhild in accusing Siegfried of having betrayed Gunther with her, a correspondence in defence of the beloved heroine was opened in The Daily Chronicle. The imputation of falsehood to Brynhild was strongly resented and combated, in spite of the unanswerable evidence of the text. It was contended that Brynhild's statement must be taken as establishing the fact that she actually was ravished by somebody whom she believed to be Siegfried, and that since this somebody cannot have been Siegfried, he being as incapable of treachery to Gunther as she of falsehood, it must have been Gunther himself after a second exchange of personalities not mentioned in the text. The reply to this—if so obviously desperate a hypothesis needs a reply—is that the text is perfectly explicit as to Siegfried, disguised as Gunther, passing the night with Brynhild with Nothung dividing them, and in the morning bringing her down the mountain THROUGH THE FIRE (an impassable obstacle to Gunther) and there transporting himself in a single breath, by the Tarnhelm's magic, back to the hall of the Gibichungs, leaving the real Gunther to bring Brynhild down the river after him. One controversialist actually pleaded for the expedition occupying two nights, on the second of which the alleged outrage might have taken place. But the time is accounted for to the last minute: it all takes place during the single night watch of Hagen. There is no possible way out of the plain fact that Brynhild's accusation is to her own knowledge false; and the impossible ways just cited are only interesting as examples of the fanatical worship which Wagner and his creations have been able to inspire in minds of exceptional power and culture.

More plausible was the line taken by those who admitted the falsehood. Their contention was that when Wotan deprived Brynhild of her Godhead, he also deprived her of her former high moral attributes; so that Siegfried's kiss awakened an ordinary mortal jealous woman. But a goddess can become mortal and jealous without plunging at once into perjury and murder. Besides, this explanation involves the sacrifice of the whole significance of the allegory, and the reduction of The Ring to the plane of a— child's conception of The Sleeping Beauty. Whoever does not understand that, in terms of The Ring philosophy, a change from godhead to humanity is a step higher and not a degradation, misses the whole point of The Ring. It is precisely because the truthfulness of Brynhild is proof against Wotan's spells that he has to contrive the fire palisade with Loki, to protect the fictions and conventions of Valhalla against her.

The only tolerable view is the one supported by the known history of The Ring, and also, for musicians of sufficiently fine judgment, by the evidence of the scores; of which more anon. As a matter of fact Wagner began, as I have said, with Siegfried's Death. Then, wanting to develop the idea of Siegfried as neoProtestant, he went on to The Young Siegfried. As a Protestant cannot be dramatically projected without a pontifical antagonist. The Young Siegfried led to The Valkyries, and that again to its preface The Rhine Gold (the preface is always written after the book is finished). Finally, of course, the whole was revised. The revision, if carried out strictly, would have involved the cuttmg out of Siegfried's Death, now become inconsistent and superfluous; and that would have involved, in turn, the facing of the fact that The Ring was no longer a Niblung epic, and really demanded modern costumes, tall hats for Tarnhelms, factories for Nibelheims, villas for Valhallas, and so on—in short, a complete confession of the extent to which the old Niblung epic had become the merest pretext and name directory in the course of Wagner's travail. But, as Wagner's most eminent English interpreter once put it to me at Bayreuth between the acts of Night Falls On The Gods, the master wanted to "Lohengrinize" again after his long abstention from opera; and Siegfried's Death (first sketched in 1848, the year before the rising in Dresden and the subsequent events which so deepened Wagner's sense of life and the seriousness of art) gave him exactly the libretto he required for that outbreak of the old operatic Adam in him. So he changed it into Die Gotterdammerung, retaining the traditional plot of murder and jealousy, and with it, necessarily, his or~gmal second act, in spite of the incongruity of its Siegfried and Brynhild with the Siegfried and Brynhild of the allegory. As to the legendary matter about the world—ash and the destruction of Valhalla by Loki, it fitted in well enough; for though, allegorically, the blow by which Siegfried breaks the god's spear is the end of Wotan and of Valhalla, those who do not see the allegory, and take the story literally, like children, are sure to ask what becomes of Wotan after Siegfried gets past him up the mountain; and to this question the old tale told in Night Falls On The Gods is as good an answer as another. The very senselessness of the scenes of the Norns and of Valtrauta in relation to the three foregoing dramas, gives them a highly effective air of mystery; and no one ventures to challenge their consequentiality, because we are all more apt to pretend to understand great works of art than to confess that the meaning (if any) has escaped us. Valtrauta, however, betrays her irrelevance by explaining that the gods can be saved by the restoration of the ring to the Rhine maidens. This, considered as part of the previous allegory, is nonsense; so that even this scene, which has a more plausible air of organic connection with The Valkyries than any other in Night Falls On The Gods, is as clearly part of a different and earlier conception as the episode which concludes it, in which Siegfried actually robs Brynhild of her ring, though he has no recollection of having given it to her. Night Falls On The Gods, in fact, was not even revised into any real coherence with the world—poem which sprang from it; and that is the authentic solution of all the controversies which have arisen over it.

The Third Act

The hunting party comes off duly. Siegfried strays from it and meets the Rhine maidens, who almost succeed in coaxing the ring from him. He pretends to be afraid of his wife; and they chaff him as to her beating him and so forth; but when they add that the ring is accursed and will bring death upon him, he discloses to them, as unconsciously as Julius Caesar disclosed it long ago, that secret of heroism, never to let your life be shaped by fear of its end.* So he keeps the ring; and they leave him to his fate. The hunting party now finds him; and they all sit down together to make a meal by the river side, Siegfried telling them meanwhile the story of his adventures. When he approaches the subject of Brynhild, as to whom his memory is a blank, Hagen pours an antidote to the love philtre into his drinking horn, whereupon, his memory returning, he proceeds to narrate the incident of the fiery mountain, to Gunther's intense mortification. Hagen then plunges his spear into the back of Siegfried, who falls dead on his shield, but gets up again, after the old operatic custom, to sing about thirty bars to his love before allowing himself to be finally carried off to the strains of the famous Trauermarsch.

*"We must learn to die, and to die in the fullest sense of the word. The fear of the end is the source of all lovelessness; and this fear is generated only when love begins to wane. How came it that this loves the highest blessedness to all things living, was so far lost sight of by the human race that at last it came to this: all that mankind did, ordered, and established, was conceived only in fear of the end? My poem sets this forth."— Wagner to Roeckel, 25th Jan. 1854.

The scene then changes to the hall of the Gibichungs by the Rhine. It is night; and Gutrune, unable to sleep, and haunted by all sorts of vague terrors, is waiting for the return of her husband, and wondering whether a ghostly figure she has seen gliding down to the river bank is Brynhild, whose room is empty. Then comes the cry of Hagen, returning with the hunting party to announce the death of Siegfried by the tusk of a wild boar. But Gutrune divines the truth; and Hagen does not deny it. Siegfried's body is brought in; Gunther claims the ring; Hagen will not suffer him to take it; they fight; and Gunther is slain. Hagen then attempts to take it; but the dead man's hand closes on it and raises itself threateningly. Then Brynhild comes; and a funeral pyre is raised whilst she declaims a prolonged scene, extremely moving and imposing, but yielding nothing to resolute intellectual criticism except a very powerful and elevated exploitation of theatrical pathos, psychologically identical with the scene of Cleopatra and the dead Antony in Shakespeare's tragedy. Finally she flings a torch into the pyre, and rides her war-horse into the flames. The hall of the Gibichungs catches fire, as most halls would were a cremation attempted in the middle of the floor (I permit myself this gibe purposely to emphasize the excessive artificiality of the scene); but the Rhine overflows its banks to allow the three Rhine maidens to take the ring from Siegfried's finger, incidentally extinguishing the conflagration as it does so. Hagen attempts to snatch the ring from the maidens, who promptly drown him; and in the distant heavens the Gods and their castle are seen perishing in the fires of Loki as the curtain falls.

FORGOTTEN ERE FINISHED

In all this, it will be observed, there is nothing new. The musical fabric is enormously elaborate and gorgeous; but you cannot say, as you must in witnessing The Rhme Gold, The Valkyries, and the first two acts of Siegfried, that you have never seen anything like it before, and that the inspiration is entirely original. Not only the action, but most of the poetry, might conceivably belong to an Elizabethan drama. The situation of Cleopatra and Antony is unconsciously reproduced without being bettered, or even equalled in point of majesty and musical expression. The loss of al! simplicity and dignity, the impossibility of any credible scenic presentation of the incidents, and the extreme staginess of the conventions by which these impossibilities are got over, are no doubt covered from the popular eye by the overwhelming prestige of Die Gotterdammerung as part of so great a work as The Ring, and by the extraordinary storm of emotion and excitement which the music keeps up. But the very qualities that intoxicate the novice in music enlighten the adept. In spite of the fulness of the composer's technical accomplishment, the finished style and effortless mastery of harmony and instrumentation displayed, there is not a bar in the work which moves us as the same themes moved us in The Valkyries, nor is anything but external splendor added to the life and humor of Siegfried.

In the original poem, Brynhild delays her self-immolation on the pyre of Siegfried to read the assembled choristers a homily on the efficacy of the Love panacea. "My holiest wisdom's hoard," she says, "now I make known to the world. I believe not in property, nor money, nor godliness, nor hearth and high place, nor pomp and peerage, nor contract and custom, but in Love. Let that only prevail; and ye shall be blest in weal or woe." Here the repudiations still smack of Bakoonin; but the saviour is no longer the volition of the full−grown spirit of Man, the Free Willer of Necessity, sword in hand, but simply Love, and not even Shelleyan love, but vehement sexual passion. It is highly significant of the extent to which this uxorious commonplace lost its hold of Wagner (after disturbing his conscience, as he confesses to Roeckel, for years) that it disappears in the full score of Night Falls On The Gods, which was not completed until he was on the verge of producing Parsifal, twenty years after the publication of the poem. He cut the homily out, and composed the music of the final scene with a flagrant recklessness of the old intention. The rigorous logic with which representative musical themes are employed in the earlier dramas is here abandoned without scruple; and for the main theme at the conclusion he selects a rapturous passage sung by Sieglinda in the third act of The Valkyries when Brynhild inspires her with a sense of her high destiny as the mother of the unborn hero. There is no dramatic logic whatever in the recurrence of this theme to express the transport in which Brynhild immolates herself. There is of course an excuse for it, inasmuch as both women have an impulse of self−sacrifice for the sake of Siegfried; but this is really hardly more than an excuse; since the Valhalla theme might be attached to Alberic on the no worse ground that both he and Wotan are inspired by ambition, and that the ambition has the same object, the possession of the ring. The common sense of the matter is that the only themes which had fully retained their significance in Wagner's memory at the period of the composition of Night Falls On The Gods are those which are mere labels of external features, such as the Dragon, the Fire, the Water and so on. This particular theme of Sieglinda's is, in truth, of no great musical merit: it might easily be the pet climax of a popular sentimental ballad: in fact, the gushing effect which is its sole valuable quality is so cheaply attained that it is hardly going too far to call it the most trumpery phrase in the entire tetralogy. Yet, since it undoubtedly does gush very emphatically, Wagner chose, for convenience' sake, to work up this final scene with it rather than with the more distinguished, elaborate and beautiful themes connected with the love of Brynhild and Siegfried.

He would certainly not have thought this a matter of no consequence had he finished the whole work ten years earlier. It must always be borne in mind that the poem of The Ring was complete and printed in 1853, and represents the sociological ideas which, after germinating in the European atmosphere for many years, had been brought home to Wagner, who was intensely susceptible to such ideas, by the crash of 1849 at Dresden. Now no man whose mind is alive and active, as Wagner's was to the day of his death, can keep his political and spiritual opinions, much less his philosophic consciousness, at a standstill for quarter of a century until he finishes an orchestral score. When Wagner first sketched Night Falls On The Gods he was 35. When he finished the score for the first Bayreuth festival in 1876 he had turned 60. No wonder he had lost his old grip of it and left it behind him. He even tampered with The Rhine Gold for the sake of theatrical effect when stage–managing it, making Wotan pick up and brandish a sword to give visible point to his sudden inspiration as to the raising up of a hero. The sword had first to be discovered by Fafnir among the Niblung treasures and thrown away by him as useless. There is no sense in this device; and its adoption shows the same recklessness as to the original intention which we find in the music of the last act of The Dusk of the Gods.*

*Die Gotterdammerung means literally Godsgloaming. The English versions of the opera are usually called The Dusk of the Gods, or The Twilight of the Gods. I have purposely introduced the ordinary title in the sentence above for the reader's information.

WHY HE CHANGED HIS MIND

Wagner, however, was not the man to allow his grip of a great philosophic theme to slacken even in twenty–five years if the theme still held good as a theory of actual life. If the history of Germany from 1849 to 1876 had been the history of Siegfried and Wotan transposed into the key of actual life Night Falls On The Gods would have been the logical consummation of Das Rheingold and The Valkyrie instead of the operatic anachronism it actually is.

But, as a matter of fact, Siegfried did not succeed and Bismarck did. Roeckel was a prisoner whose mposonment made no difference; Bakoonin broke up, not Walhall, but the International, which ended in an undignified quarrel between him and Karl Marx. The Siegfrieds of 1848 were hopeless political failures, whereas the Wotans and Alberics and Lows were conspicuous political successes. Even the Mimes held their own as against Siegfried. With the single exception of Ferdinand Lassalle, there was no revolutionary leader who was not an obvious impossibilist in practical politics; and Lassalle got himself killed in a romantic and quite indefensible duel after wrecking his health in a titanic oratorical campaign which convinced him that the great majority of the working classes were not ready to join him, and that the minority who were ready did not understand him. The International, founded in 1861 by Karl Marx in London, and mistaken for several years by nervous newspapers for a red spectre, was really only a turnip ghost. It achieved some beginnings of International Trade Unionism by inducing English workmen to send money to support strikes on the continent, and recalling English workers who had been taken across the North Sea to defeat such strikes; but on its revolutionary socialistic side it was a romantic figment. The suppression of the Paris Commune, one of the most tragic examples in history of the pitilessness with which capable practical administrators and soldiers are forced by the pressure of facts to destroy romantic amateurs and theatrical dreamers, made an end of melodramatic Socialism. It was as easy for Marx to hold up Thiers as the most execrable of living scoundrels and to put upon Gallifet the brand that still makes him impossible in French politics as it was for Victor Hugo to bombard Napoleon III from his paper battery in Jersey. It was also easy to hold up Felix Pyat and Delescluze as men of much loftier ideals than Thiers and Gallifet; but the one fact that could not be denied was that when it came to actual shooting, it was Gallifet who got Delescluze shot and not Delescluze who got Gallifet shot, and that when it came to administering the affairs of France, Thiers could in one way or another get it done, whilst Pyat could neither do it nor stop talking and allow somebody else to do it. True, the penalty of following Thiers was to be exploited by the landlord and capitalist; but then the penalty of following Pyat was to get shot like a mad dog, or at best get sent to New Caledonia, quite unnecessarily and uselessly.

To put it in terms of Wagner's allegory, Alberic had got the ring back again and was marrying into the best Walhall families with it. He had thought better of his old threat to dethrone Wotan and Loki. He had found that Nibelheim was a very gloomy place and that if he wanted to live handsomely and safely, he must not only allow Wotan and Loki to organize society for him, but pay them very handsomely for doing it. He wanted splendor, military glory, loyalty, enthusiasm, and patriotism; and his greed and gluttony were wholly unable to create them, whereas Wotan and Loki carried them all to a triumphant climax in Germany in 1871, when Wagner himself celebrated the event with his Kaisermarsch, which sounded much more convincing than the Marseillaise or the Carmagnole.

How, after the Kaisermarsch, could Wagner go back to his idealization of Siegfried in 1853? How could he believe seriously in Siegfried slaying the dragon and charging through the mountain fire, when the immediate foreground was occupied by the Hotel de Ville with Felix Pyat endlessly discussing the principles of Socialism whilst the shells of Thiers were already battering the Arc de Triomphe, and ripping up the pavement of the

Champs Elysees? Is it not clear that things had taken an altogether unexpected turn—that although the Ring may, like the famous Communist Manifesto of Marx and Engels, be an inspired guest at the historic laws and predestined end of our capitalistic–theocratic epoch, yet Wagner, like Marx, was too inexperienced in technical government and administration and too melodramatic in his hero–contra–villain conception of the class struggle, to foresee the actual process by which his generalization would work out, or the part to be played in it by the classes involved?

Let us go back for a moment to the point at which the Niblung legend first becomes irreconcilable with Wagner's allegory. Fafnir in the allegory becomes a capitalist; but Fafnir in the legend is a mere hoarder. His gold does not bring him in any revenue. It does not even support him: he has to go out and forage for food and drink. In fact, he is on the way to his drinking–pool when Siegfried kills him. And Siegfried himself has no more use for gold than Fafnir: the only difference between them in this respect is that Siegfried does not waste his time in watching a barren treasure that is no use to him, whereas Fafnir sacrifices his humanity and his life merely to prevent anybody else getting it. This contrast is true to human nature; but it shunts The Ring drama off the economic lines of the allegory. In real life, Fafnir is not a miser: he seeks dividends, comfortable life, and admission to the circles of Wotan and Loki. His only means of procuring these is to restore the gold to Alberic in exchange for scrip in Alberic's enterprises. Thus fortified with capital, Alberic exploits his fellow dwarfs as before, and also exploits Fafair's fellow giants who have no capital. What is more, the toil, forethought and self–control which the exploitation involves, and the self–respect and social esteem which its success wins, effect an improvement in Alberic's own character which neither Marx nor Wagner appear to have foreseen. He discovers that to be a dull, greedy, narrow–minded money–grubber is not the way to make money on a large scale; for though greed may suffice to turn tens into hundreds and even hundreds into thousands, to turn thousands into hundreds of thousands requires magnanimity and a will to power rather than to pelf. And to turn thousands into millions, Alberic must make himself an earthly providence for masses of workmen: he must create towns and govern markets. In the meantime, Fafair, wallowing in dividends which he has done nothing to earn, may rot, intellectually and morally, from mere disuse of his energies and lack of incentive to excel; but the more imbecile he becomes, the more dependent he is upon Alberic, and the more the responsibility of keeping the world–machine in working order falls upon Alberic. Consequently, though Alberic in Also may have been merely the vulgar Manchester Factory–owner portrayed by Engels, in 1876 he was well on the way towards becoming Krupp of Essen or

Carnegie of Homestead.

Now, without exaggerating the virtues of these gentlemen, it will be conceded by everybody except perhaps those veteran German Social–Democrats who have made a cult of obsolescence under the name of Marxism, that the modern entrepreneur is not to be displaced and dismissed so lightly as Alberic is dismissed in The Ring. They are really the masters of the whole situation. Wotan is hardly less dependent on them than Fafnir; the War–Lord visits their work, acclaims them in stirring speeches, and casts down their enemies; whilst Loki makes commercial treaties for them and subjects all his diplomacy to their approval.

The end cannot come until Siegfried learns Alberic's trade and shoulders Alberic's burden. Not having as yet done so, he is still completely mastered by Alberic. He does not even rebel against him except when he is too stupid and ignorant, or too romantically impracticable, to see that Alberic's work, like Wotan's work and Loki's work, is necessary work, and that therefore Alberic can never be superseded by a warrior, but only by a capable man of business who is prepared to continue his work without a day's intermission. Even though the proletarians of all lands were to become "class conscious," and obey the call of Marx by uniting to carry the Class struggle to a proletarian victory in which all capital should become common property, and all Monarchs, Millionaires, Landlords and Capitalists become common citizens, the triumphant proletarians would have either to starve in Anarchy the next day or else do the political and industrial work which is now being done tant bien que mal by our Romanoffs, our Hohenzollerns, our Krupps, Carnegies, Levers, Pierpont Morgans, and their political retinues. And in the meantime these magnates must defend their power and property with all their might against the revolutionary forces until these forces become positive, executive, administrative forces, instead of the conspiracies of protesting, moralizing, virtuously indignant amateurs who mistook Marx for a man of affairs and Thiers for a stage villain. But all this represents a development of which one gathers no forecast from Wagner or Marx. Both of them prophesied the end of our epoch, and, so far as one can guess, prophesied it rightly. They also brought its industrial history up to the year 1848 far more penetratingly than the academic historians of their time. But they broke off there and left a void between 1848 and the end, in which we, who have to live in that period, get no guidance from them. The Marxists wandered for years in this void, striving, with fanatical superstition, to suppress the Revisionists who, facing the fact that the Social–Democratic party was lost, were trying to find the path by the light of contemporary history instead of vainly consulting the oracle in the pages of Das Kapital. Marx himself was too simpleminded a recluse and too full of the validity of his remoter generalizations, and the way in which the rapid integration of capital in Trusts and Kartels was confirming them, to be conscious of the void himself.

Wagner, on the other hand, was comparatively a practical man. It is possible to learn more of the world by producing a single opera, or even conductmg a single orchestral rehearsal, than by ten years reading in the Library of the British Museum. Wagner must have learnt between Das Rheingold and the Kaisermarsch that there are yet several dramas to be interpolated in The Ring after The Valkyries before the allegory can tell the whole story, and that the first of these interpolated dramas will be much more like a revised Rienzi than like Siegfried. If anyone doubts the extent to which Wagner's eyes had been opened to the administrative–childishness and romantic conceit of the heroes of the revolutionary generation that served its apprenticeship on the barricades of 1848–9, and perished on those of 187@ under Thiers' mitrailleuses, let him read Eine Kapitulation, that scandalous burlesque in which the poet and composer of Siegfried, with the levity of a schoolboy, mocked the French republicans who were doing in 1871 what he himself was exiled for domg in 1849. He had set the enthusiasm of the Dresden Revolution to his own greatest music; but he set the enthusiasm of twenty years later in derision to the music of Rossini. There is no mistaking the tune he meant to suggest by his doggerel of Republik, Republik, Republik–lik–lik. The Overture to Wilhelm Tell is there as plainly as if it were noted down in full score.

In the case of such a man as Wagner, you cannot explain this volte–face as mere jingoism produced by Germany's overwhelming victory in the Franco–Prussian War, nor as personal spite against the Parisians for the Tannhauser fiasco. Wagner had more cause for personal spite against his own countrymen than he ever had against the French. No doubt his outburst gratified the pettier feelings which great men have in common with small ones; but he was not a man to indulge in such gratifications, or indeed to feel them as gratifications, if he had not arrived at a profound philosophical contempt for the inadequacy of the men who were trying to wield Nothung, and who had done less work for Wagner's own art than a single German King and he, too, only a mad one. Wagner had by that time done too much himself not to know that the world is ruled by deeds, not by good intentions, and that one efficient sinner is worth ten futile saints and martyrs.

I need not elaborate the point further in these pages. Like all men of genius, Wagner had exceptional sincerity, exceptional respect for facts, exceptional freedom from the hypnotic influence of sensational popular movements, exceptional sense of the realities of political power as distinguished from the presences and idolatries behind which the real masters of modern States pull their wires and train their guns. When he scored Night Falls On The Gods, he had accepted the failure of Siegfried and the triumph of the Wotan–Loki–Alberic–trinity as a fact. He had given up dreaming of heroes, heroines, and final solutions, and had conceived a new protagonist in Parsifal, whom he announced, not as a hero, but as a fool; who was armed, not with a sword which cut irresistibly, but with a spear which he held only on condition that he did not use it; and who instead of exulting in the slaughter of a dragon was frightfully ashamed of having shot a swan. The change in the conception of the Deliverer could hardly be more complete. It reflects the change which took place in Wagner's mind between the composition of The Rhine Gold and Night Falls On The Gods; and it explains why he dropped The Ring allegory and fell back on the status quo ante by Lohengrinizing.

If you ask why he did not throw Siegfried into the waste paper basket and rewrite The Ring from The Valkyries onwards, one must reply that the time had not come for such a feat. Neither Wagner nor anyone else then living knew enough to achieve it. Besides, what he had already done had reached the omit of even his immense energy and perseverance and so he did the best he could with the unfinished and for ever unfinishable work, rounding it off with an opera much as Rossini rounded off some of his religious compositions with a galop. Only, Rossini on such occasions wrote in his score "Excusez du pen," but Wagner left us to find out the change for ourselves, perhaps to test how far we had really followed his meaning.

WAGNER'S OWN EXPLANATION

And now, having given my explanation of The Ring, can I give Wagner's explanation of it? If I could (and I can) I should not by any means accept it as conclusive. Nearly half a century has passed smce the tetralogy was written; and in that time the purposes of many half instinctive acts of genius have become clearer to the common man than they were to the doers. Some years ago, in the course of an explanation of Ibsen's plays, I pointed out that it was by no means certain or even likely that Ibsen was as definitely conscious of his thesis as I. All the stupid people, and some critics who, though not stupid, had not themselves written what the Germans call "tendency" works, saw nothing in this but a fantastic affectation of the extravagant self–conceit of knowing more about Ibsen than Ibsen himself. Fortunately, in taking exactly the same position now with regard to Wagner, I can claim his own authority to support me. "How," he wrote to Roeckel on the 23rd. August 1856, "can an artist expect that what he has felt intuitively should be perfectly realized by others, seeing that he himself feels in the presence of his work, if it is true Art, that he is confronted by a riddle, about which he, too, might have illusions, just as another might?"

The truth is, we are apt to deify men of genius, exactly as we deify the creative force of the universe, by attributing to logical design what is the result of blind instinct. What Wagner meant by "true Art" is the operation of the artist's instinct, which is just as blind as any other instinct. Mozart, asked for an explanation of his works, said frankly "How do I know?" Wagner, being a philosopher and critic as well as a composer, was always looking for moral explanations of what he had created) and he hit on several very striking ones, all different. In the same way one can conceive Henry the Eighth speculating very brilliantly about the circulation of his own blood without getting as near the truth as Harvey did long after his death.

None the less, Wagner's own explanations are of exceptional interest. To begin with, there is a considerable portion of The Ring, especially the portraiture of our capitalistic industrial system from the socialist's point of new in the slavery of the Niblungs and the tyranny of Alberic, which is unmistakable, as it dramatizes that portion of human activity which lies well within the territory covered by our intellectual consciousness. All this is concrete Home Office business, so to speak: its meaning was as clear to Wagner as it is to us. Not so that part of the work which deals with the destiny of Wotan. And here, as it happened, Wagner's recollection of what he had been driving at was completely upset by his discovery, soon after the completion of The Ring poem, of Schopenhaur's famous treatise "The World as Will and Representation." So obsessed did he become with this masterpiece of philosophic art that he declared that it contained the intellectual demonstration of the conflict of human forces which he himself had demonstrated artistically in his great poem. "I must confess," he writes to Roeckel, "to having arrived at a clear understanding of my own works of art through the help of another, who has provided me with the reasoned conceptions corresponding to my intuitive principles."

Schopenhaur, however, had done nothing of the sort. Wagner's determination to prove that he had been a Schopenhaurite all along without knowing it only shows how completely the fascination of the great treatise on The Will had run away with his memory. It is easy to see how this happened. Wagner says of himself that "seldom has there taken place in the soul of one and the same man so profound a division and estrangement between the intuitive or impulsive part of his nature and his consciously or reasonably formed ideas." And since Schopenhaur's great contribution to modern thought was to educate us into clear consciousness of this distinction—a distinction familiar, in a fanciful way, to the Ages of Faith and Art before the Renascence, but afterwards swamped in the Rationalism of that movement—it was inevitable that Wagner should jump at Schopenhaur's metaphysiology (I use a word less likely to be mistaken than metaphysics) as the very thing for him. But metaphysiology is one thing, political philosophy another. The political philosophy of Siegfried is exactly contrary to the political philosphy of Schopenhaur, although the same clear metaphysiological distinction between the instinctive part of man (his Will) and his reasoning faculty (dramatized in The Ring as Loki) is insisted on in both. The difference is that to Schopenhaur the Will is the universal tormentor of man, the author of that great evil, Life; whilst reason is the divine gift that is finally to overcome this life–creating will and lead, through its aboegation, to cessation and peace, annihilation and Nirvana. This is the doctrine of Pessimism. Now Wagner was, when he wrote The Ring, a most sanguine revolutionary Meliorist, contemptuous of the reasoning faculty, which he typified in the shifty, unreal, delusive Loki, and full of faith in the life–giving Will, which he typified in the glorious Siegfried. Not until he read Schopenhaur did he become bent on proving that he had always been a Pessimist at heart, and that Loki was the most sensible and worthy adviser of Wotan in The Rhine Gold.

Sometimes he faces the change in his opinions frankly enough. "My Niblung drama," he writes to Roeckel, "had taken form at a time when I had built up with my reason an optimistic world on Hellenic principles, believing that nothing was necessary for the realization of such a world but that men should wish it. I ingeniously set aside–the problem why they did not wish it. I remember that it was with this definite creative purpose that I conceived the personality of Siegfried, with the intention of representing an existence free from pain." But he appeals to his earlier works to show that behind all these artificial optimistic ideas there was always with him an intuition of "the sublime tragedy of renunciation, the negation of the will." In trying to explain this, he s full of ideas philosophically, and full of the most amusing contradictions personally. Optimism, as an accidental excursion into the barren paths of reason on his own part, he calls "Hellenic." In others he denounces it as rank Judaism, the Jew having at that time become for him the whipping boy for all modern humamty. In a letter from London he expounds Schopenhaur to Roeckel with enthusiasm, preaching the renunciation of the Will to Live as the redemption from all error and vain pursuits: in the next letter he resumes the subject with unabated interest, and fin~shes by mentioning that on leaving London he went to Geneva and underwent "a most beneficial course of hydropathy." Seven months before this he had written as follows: "Believe me, I too was once possessed by the idea of a country life. In order to become a radically healthy human being, I went two years ago to a Hydropathic Establishment, prepared to give up Art and everything f I could once more become a child of Nature. But, my good friend, I was obliged to laugh at my own naivete when I found myself almost going mad. None of us will reach the promised land: we shall all die in the wilderness. Intellect is, as some one has said, a sort of disease: it is incurable.

Roeckel knew his man of old, and evidently pressed him for explanations of the inconsistencies of The Ring with Night Falls On The Gods. Wagner defended himself with unfailing cleverness and occasional petulances, ranging from such pleas as "I believe a true instinct has kept me from a too great definiteness; for it has been borne in on me that an absolute disclosure of the intention disturbs true insight," to a volley of explanations and commentaries on the explanations. He gets excited and annoyed because Roeckel will not admire the Brynhild of Night Falls On The Gods; re–invents the Tarnhelm scene; and finally, the case being desperate, exclaims, "It is wrong of you to challenge me to explain it in words: you must feel that something is being enacted that is not to be expressed in mere words."

THE PESSIMIST AS AMORIST

Sometimes he gets very far away from Pessimism indeed, and recommends Roeckel to solace his captivity, not by conquering the will to live at liberty, but by "the inspiring influences of the Beautiful." The next moment he throws over even Art for Life. "Where life ends," he says, very wittily, "Art begins. In youth we turn to Art, we know not why; and only when we have gone through with Art and come out on the other side, we learn to our cost that we have missed Life itself." His only comfort is that he is beloved. And on the subject of love he lets himself loose in a manner that would have roused the bitterest scorn in Schopenhaur, though, as we have seen (Love Panacea), it is highly characteristic of Wagner. "Love in its most perfect reality," he says, "is only possible between the sexes: it is only as man and woman that human beings can truly love. Every other manifestation of love can be traced back to that one absorbingly real feeling, of which all other affections are but an emanation, a connection, or an imitation. It is an error to look on this as only one of the forms in which love is revealed, as if there were other forms coequal with it, or even superior to it. He who after the manner of metaphysicians prefers UNREALITY to REALITY, and derives the concrete from the abstract—in short, puts the word before the fact—may be right in esteeming the idea of love as higher than the expression of love, and may affirm that actual love made manifest in feeling is nothing but the outward and visible sign of a pre—existent, non—sensuous, abstract love; and he will do well to despise that sensuous function in general. In any case it were safe to bet that such a man had never loved or been loved as human beings can love, or he would have understood that in despising this feeling, what he condemned was its sensual expression, the outcome of man's animal nature, and not true human love. The highest satisfaction and expression of the individual is only to be found in his complete absorption, and that is only possible through love. Now a human being is both MAN and WOMAN: it is only when these two are united that the real human being exists; and thus it is only by love that man and woman attain to the full measure of humanity. But when nowadays we talk of a human being, such heartless blockheads are we that quite involuntarily we only think of man. It is only in the umon of man and woman by love (sensuous and supersensuous) that the human being exists; and as the human being cannot rise to the conception of anything higher than his own existence—his own being—so the transcendent act of his life is this consummation of his humanity through love."

It is clear after this utterance from the would—be Schopenhaurian, that Wagner's explanations of his works for the most part explain nothing but the mood in which he happened to be on the day he advanced them, or the train of thought suggested to his very susceptible imagination and active mind by the points raised by his questioner. Especially in his private letters, where his outpourings are modified by his dramatic consciousness of the personality of his correspondent, do we find him taking all manner of positions, and putting forward all sorts of cases which must be taken as clever and suggestive special pleadings, and not as serious and permanent expositions of his works. These works must speak for themselves: if The Ring says one thing, and a letter written afterwards says that it said something else, The Ring must be taken to confute the letter just as conclusively as if the two had been written by different hands. However, nobody fairly well acquainted with Wagner's utterances as a whole will find any unaccountable contradictions in them. As in all men of his type, our manifold nature was so marked in him that he was like several different men rolled into one. When he had exhausted himself in the character of the most pugnacious, aggressive, and sanguine of reformers, he rested himself as a Pessimist and Ninanist. In The Ring the quietism of Brynhild's "Rest, rest, thou God" is sublime in its deep conviction; but you have only to turn back the pages to find the irrepressible bustle of Siegfried and the revelry of the clansmen expressed with equal zest. Wagner was not a Schopenhaurite every day in the week, nor even a Wagnerite. His mind changes as often as his mood. On Monday nothing will ever induce him to return to quilldriving: on Tuesday he begins a new pamphlet. On Wednesday he is impatient of the misapprehensions of people who cannot see how impossible it is for him to preside as a conductor over platform performances of fragments of his works, which can only be understood when presented strictly according to his intention on the stage: on Thursday he gets up a concert of Wagnerian selections, and when it is over writes to his friends describing how profoundly both bandsmen and audience were impressed. On Friday he exults in the self–assertion of Siegfried's will against all moral ordinances, and is full of a revolutionary sense of "the universal law of change and renewal": on Saturday he has an attack of holiness, and asks, "Can you conceive a moral action of which the root idea is not renunciation?" In short, Wagner can be quoted against himself almost without limit, much as Beethoven's adagios could be quoted against his scherzos if a dispute arose between two fools as to whether he was a melancholy man or a merry one.

THE MUSIC OF THE RING

THE REPRESENTATIVE THEMES

To be able to follow the music of The Ring, all that is necessary is to become familiar enough with the brief musical phrases out of which it is built to recognize them and attach a certain definite significance to them, exactly as any ordinary Englishman recognizes and attaches a definite significance to the opening bars of God Save the King. There is no difficulty here: every soldier is expected to learn and distinguish between different bugle calls and trumpet calls; and anyone who can do this can learn and distinguish between the representative themes or "leading motives" (Leitmotifs) of The Ring. They are the easier to learn because they are repeated agam and agam; and the main ones are so emphatically impressed on the ear whilst the spectator is looking for the first time at the objects, or witnessing the first strong dramatic expression of the ideas they denote, that the requisite association is formed unconsciously. The themes are neither long, nor complicated, nor difficult. Whoever can pick up the flourish of a coach–horn, the note of a bird, the rhythm of the postman's knock or of a horse's gallop, will be at no loss in picking up the themes of The Ring. No doubt, when it comes to forming the necessary mental association with the theme, it may happen that the spectator may find his ear conquering the tune more easily than his mind conquers the thought. But for the most part the themes do not denote thoughts at all, but either emotions of a quite simple universal kind, or the sights, sounds and fancies common enough to be familiar to children. Indeed some of them are as frankly childish as any of the funny little orchestral interludes which, in Haydn's Creation, introduce the horse, the deer, or the worm. We have both the horse and the worm in The Ring, treated exactly in Haydn's manner, and with an effect not a whit less ridiculous to superior people who decline to take it good–humoredly. Even the complaisance of good Wagnerites is occasionally rather overstrained by the way in which Brynhild's allusions to her charger Grani elicit from the band a little rum–ti–tum triplet which by itself is in no way suggestive of a horse, although a continuous rush of such triplets makes a very exciting musical gallop.

Other themes denote objects which cannot be imitatively suggested by music: for instance, music cannot suggest a ring, and cannot suggest gold; yet each of these has a representative theme which pervades the score in all directions. In the case of the gold the association is established by the very salient way in which the orchestra breaks into the pretty theme in the first act of The Rhine Gold at the moment when the sunrays strike down through the water and light up the glittering treasure, "hitherto invisible. The reference of the strange little theme of the wishing cap is equally manifest from the first, since the spectator's attention is wholly taken up with the Tarnhelm and its magic when the theme is first pointedly uttered by the orchestra. The sword theme is introduced at the end of The Rhine Gold to express Wotan's hero inspiration; and I have already mentioned that Wagner, unable, when it came to practical stage management, to forego the appeal to the eye as well as to the thought, here made Wotan pick up a sword and brandish it, though no such instruction appears in the printed score. When this sacrifice to Wagner's scepticism as to the reality of any appeal to an audience that is not made through their bodily sense is omitted, the association of the theme with the sword is not formed until that point in the first act of The Valkyries at which Siegmund is left alone by Hunding's hearth, weaponless, with the assurance that he will have to fight for his life at dawn with his host. He recalls then how his father promised him a sword for his hour of need; and as he does so, a flicker from the dying fire is caught by the golden hilt of the sword in the tree, when the theme immediately begins to gleam through the quiver of sound from the orchestra, and only dies out as the fire sinks and the sword is once more hidden by the darkness. Later on, this theme, which is never silent whilst Sieglinda is dwelling on the story of the sword, leaps out into the most dazzling splendor the band can give it when Siegmund triumphantly draws the weapon from the tree. As it consists of seven notes only, with a very marked measure, and a melody like a simple flourish on a trumpet or post horn, nobody capable of catching a tune can easily miss it.

The Valhalla theme, sounded with solemn grandeur as the home of the gods first appears to us and to Wotan at the beginning of the second scene of The Rhine Gold, also cannot be mistaken. It, too, has a memorable rhythm; and its majestic harmonies, far from presenting those novel or curious problems in polyphony of which Wagner still stands suspected by superstitious people, are just those three simple chords which festive students who vamp accompaniments to comic songs "by ear" soon find sufficient for nearly all the popular tunes in the world.

On the other hand, the ring theme, when it begins to hurtle through the third scene of The Rhine Gold, cannot possibly be referred to any special feature in the general gloom and turmoil of the den of the dwarfs. It is not a melody, but merely the displaced metric accent which musicians call syncopation, rung on the notes of the familiar chord formed by piling three minor thirds on top of one another (technically, the chord of the minor ninth, ci–devant diminished seventh). One soon picks it up and identifies it; but it does not get introduced in the unequivocally clear fashion of the themes described above, or of that malignant monstrosity, the theme which denotes the curse on the gold. Consequently it cannot be said that the musical design of the work is perfectly clear at the first hearing as regards all the themes; but it is so as regards most of them, the main lines being laid down as emphatically and intelligibly as the dramatic motives in a Shakespearean play. As to the coyer subtleties of the score, their discovery provides fresh interest for repeated hearings, giving The Ring a Beethovenian inexhaustibility and toughness of wear.

The themes associated with the individual characters get stamped on the memory easily by the simple association of the sound of the theme with the appearance of the person indicated. Its appropriateness is generally pretty obvious. Thus, the entry of the giants Is made to a vigorous stumping, tramping measure. Mimmy, being a quaint, weird old creature, has a quaint, weird theme of two thin chords that creep down eerily one to the other. Gutrune's theme is pretty and caressing: Gunther's bold, rough, and commonplace. It is a favorite trick of Wagner's, when one of his characters is killed on the stage, to make the theme attached to that character weaken, fail, and fade away with a broken echo into silence.

THE CHARACTERIZATION

All this, however, is the mere child's play of theme work. The more complex characters, instead of having a simple musical label attached to them, have their characteristic ideas and aspirations identified with special representative themes as they come into play in the drama; and the chief merit of the thematic structure of The Ring is the mastery with which the dramatic play of the ideas is reflected in the contrapuntal play of the themes. We do not find Wotan, like the dragon or the horse, or, for the matter of that, like the stage demon in Weber's Freischutz or Meyerbeer's Robert the Devil, with one fixed theme attached to him like a name plate to an umbrella, blaring unaltered from the orchestra whenever he steps on the stage. Sometimes we have the Valhalla theme used to express the greatness of the gods as an idea of Wotan's. Again, we have his spear, the symbol of his power, identified with another theme, on which Wagner finally exercises his favorite device by making it break and fail, cut through, as it were, by the tearing sound of the theme identified with the sword, when Siegfried shivers the spear with the stroke of Nothung. Yet another theme connected with Wotan is the Wanderer music which breaks with such a majestic reassurance on the nightmare terror of Mimmy when Wotan appears at the mouth of his cave in the scene of the three riddles. Thus not only are there several Wotan themes, but each varies in its inflexions and shades of tone color according to its dramatic circumstances. So, too, the merry ham tune of the young Siegfried changes its measure, loads itself with massive harmonies, and becomes an exordium of the most imposing splendor when it heralds his entry as full-fledged hero in the prologue to Night Falls On The Gods. Even Mimmy has his two or three themes: the weird one already described; the little one in triple measure imitating the tap of his hammer, and fiercely mocked in the savage laugh of Alberic at his death; and finally the crooning tune in which he details all his motherly kindnesses to the little foundling Siegfried. Besides this there are all manner of little musical blinkings and shamblings and whinings, the least hint of which from the orchestra at any moment instantly brings Mimmy to mind, whether he is on the stage at the time or not.

In truth, dramatic characterization in music cannot be carried very far by the use of representative themes. Mozart, the greatest of all masters of this art, never dreamt of employing them; and, extensively as they are used in The Ring, they do not enable Wagner to dispense with the Mozartian method. Apart from the themes, Siegfried and Mimmy are still as sharply distinguished from one another by the character of their music as Don Giovanni from Leporello, Wotan from Gutrune as Sarastro from Papagena. It is true that the themes attached to the characters have the same musical appropriateness as the rest of the music: for example, neither the Valhalla nor the spear themes could, without the most ludicrous incongruity, be used for the forest bird or the unstable, delusive Loki; but for all that the musical characterization must be regarded as independent of the specific themes, since the entire elimination of the thematic system from the score would leave the characters as well distinguished musically as they are at present.

One more illustration of the way in which the thematic system is worked. There are two themes connected with Loki. One is a rapid, sinuous, twisting, shifty semiquaver figure suggested by the unsubstantial, elusive logic–spinning of the clever one's braincraft. The other is the fire theme. In the first act of Siegfried, Mimmy makes his unavailing attempt to explain fear to Siegfried. With the horror fresh upon him of the sort of nightmare into which he has fallen after the departure of the Wanderer, and which has taken the form, at once fanciful and symbolic, of a delirious dread of light, he asks Siegfried whether he has never, whilst wandering in the forest, had his heart set hammering in frantic dread by the mysterious lights of the gloaming. To this, Siegfried, greatly astonished, replies that on such occasions his heart is altogether healthy and his sensations perfectly normal Here Mimmy's question is accompanied by the tremulous sounding of the fire theme with its harmonies most oppressively disturbed and troubled; whereas with Siegfried's reply they become quite clear and straightforward, making the theme sound bold, brilliant, and serene. This is a typical instance of the way in which the themes are used.

The thematic system gives symphonic interest, reasonableness, and unity to the music, enabling the composer to exhaust every aspect and quality of his melodic material, and, in Beethoven's manner, to work miracles of beauty, expression and significance with the briefest phrases. As a set–off against this, it has led Wagner to indulge in repetitions that would be intolerable in a purely dramatic work. Almost the first thing that a dramatist has to learn in constructing a play is that the persons must not come on the stage in the second act and tell one another at great length what the audience has already seen pass before its eyes in the first act. The extent to which Wagner has been seduced into violating this rule by his affection for his themes is startling to a practiced playwright. Siegfried inherits from Wotan a mania for autobiography which leads him to inflict on every one he meets the story of Mimmy and the dragon, although the audience have spent a whole evening witnessing the events he is narrating. Hagen tells the story to Gunther; and that same night Alberic's ghost tells it over again to Hagen, who knows it already as well as the audience. Siegfried tells the Rhine maidens as much of it as they will listen to, and then keeps telling it to his hunting companions until they kill him. Wotan's autobiography on the second evening becomes his biography in the mouths of the Norns on the fourth. The little that the Norns add to it is repeated an hour later by Valtrauta. How far all this repetition is tolerable is a matter of individual taste. A good story will bear repetition; and if it has woven into it such pretty tunes as the Rhine maidens' yodel, Mimmy's tinkling anvil beat, the note of the forest bird, the call of Siegfried's horn, and so on, it will bear a good deal of rehearing. Those who have but newly learnt their way through The Ring will not readily admit that there is a bar too much repetition.

But how if you find some anti–Wagnerite raising the question whether the thematic system does not enable the composer to produce a music drama with much less musical fertility than was required from his predecessors for the composition of operas under the old system!

Such discussions are not within the scope of this little book. But as the book is now finished (for really nothing more need be said about The Ring), I am quite willing to add a few pages of ordinary musical criticism, partly to please the amateurs who enjoy that sort of reading, and partly for the guidance of those who wish to obtain some hints to help them through such critical small talk about Wagner and Bayreuth as may be forced upon them at the dinner table or between the acts.

THE OLD AND THE NEW MUSIC

In the old–fashioned opera every separate number involved the composition of a fresh melody; but it is quite a mistake to suppose that this creative–effort extended continuously throughout the number from the first to the last bar. When a musician composes according to a set metrical pattern, the selection of the pattern and the composition of the first stave (a stave in music corresponds to a line in verse) generally completes the creative effort. All the rest follows more or less mechanically to fill up the pattern, an air being very like a wall–paper design in this respect. Thus the second stave is usually a perfectly obvious consequence of the first; and the third and fourth an exact or very slightly varied repetition of the first and second. For example, given the first line of Pop Goes the Weasel or Yankee Doodle, any musical cobbler could supply the remaining three. There is very little tune turning of this kind in The Ring; and it is noteworthy that where it does occur, as in Siegmund's spring song and Mimmy's croon, "Ein zullendes Kind," the effect of the symmetrical staves, recurring as a mere matter of form, is perceptibly poor and platitudinous compared with the free flow of melody which prevails elsewhere.

The other and harder way of composing is to take a strain of free melody, and ring every variety of change of mood upon it as if it were a thought that sometimes brought hope, sometimes melancholy, sometimes exultation, sometimes raging despair and so on. To take several themes of this kind, and weave them together into a rich musical fabric passing panoramically before the ear with a continually varying flow of sentiment, is the highest feat of the musician: it is in this way that we get the fugue of Bach and the symphony of Beethoven. The admittedly inferior musician is the one who, like Auber and Offenbach, not to mention our purveyors of drawing–room ballads, can produce an unlimited quantity of symmetrical tunes, but cannot weave themes symphonically.

When this is taken into account, it will be seen that the fact that there is a great deal of repetition in The Ring does not distinguish it from the old–fashioned operas. The real difference is that in them the repetition was used for the mechanical completion of conventional metric patterns, whereas in The Ring the recurrence of the theme is an intelligent and interesting consequence of the recurrence of the dramatic phenomenon which it denotes. It should be remembered also that the substitution of symphonically treated themes for tunes with symmetrical eight–bar staves and the like, has always been the rule in the highest forms of music. To describe it, or be affected by it, as an abandonment of melody, is to confess oneself an ignoramus conversant only with dance tunes and ballads.

The sort of stuff a purely dramatic musician produces when he hampers himself with metric patterns in composition is not unlike what might have resulted in literature if Carlyle (for example) had been compelled by convention to write his historical stories in rhymed stanzas. That is to say, it limits his fertility to an occasional phrase, and three quarters of the time exercises only his barren ingenuity in fitting rhymes and measures to it. In literature the great masters of the art have long emancipated themselves from metric patterns. Nobody claims that the hierarchy of modern impassioned prose writers, from Bunyan to Ruskin, should be placed below the writers of pretty lyrics, from Herrick to Mr. Austin Dobson. Only in dramatic literature do we find the devastating tradition of blank verse still lingering, giving factitious prestige to the platitudes of dullards, and robbing the dramatic style of the genuine poet of its full natural endowment of variety, force and simplicity.

This state of things, as we have seen, finds its parallel in musical art, since music can be written in prose themes or in versified tunes; only here nobody dreams of disputing the greater difficulty of the prose forms, and the comparative triviality of versification. Yet in dramatic music, as in dramatic literature, the tradition of versification clings with the same pernicious results; and the opera, like the tragedy, is conventionally made like a wall paper. The theatre seems doomed to be in all things the last refuge of the hankering after cheap prettiness in art.

Unfortunately this confusion of the decorative with the dramatic element in both literature and music is maintained by the example of great masters in both arts. Very touching dramatic expression can be combined with decorative symmetry of versification when the artist happens to possess both the decorative and dramatic gifts, and to have cultivated both hand in hand. Shakespeare and Shelley, for instance, far from being hampered by the conventional obligation to write their dramas in verse, found it much the easiest and cheapest way of producing them. But if Shakespeare had been compelled by custom to write entirely in prose, all his ordinary dialogue might have been as good as the first scene of As You Like It; and all his lofty passages as fine as "What a piece of work is Man!", thus sparing us a great deal of blank verse in which the thought is commonplace, and the expression, though catchingly turned, absurdly pompous. The Cent might either have been a serious drama or might never have been written at all if Shelley had not been allowed to carry off its unreality by Elizabethan versification. Still, both poets have achieved many passages in which the decorative and dramatic qualities are not only reconciled, but seem to enhance one another to a pitch otherwise unattainable.

Just so in music. When we find, as in the case of Mozart, a prodigiously gifted and arduously trained musician who is also, by a happy accident, a dramatist comparable to

Mohere, the obligation to compose operas in versified numbers not only does not embarrass him, but actually saves him trouble and thought. No matter what his dramatic mood may be, he expresses it in exquisite musical verses more easily than a dramatist of ordinary singleness of talent can express it in prose. Accordingly, he too, like Shakespeare and Shelley,leaves versified airs, like Dalla sua pace, or Gluck's Che fare senza Euridice, or Weber's Leise, leise, which are as dramatic from the first note to the last as the untrammelled themes of The Ring. In consequence, it used to be professorially demanded that all dramatic music should present the same double aspect. The demand was unreasonable, since symmetrical versification is no merit in dramatic music: one might as well stipulate that a dinner fork should be constructed so as to serve also as a tablecloth. It was an ignorant demand too, because it is not true that the composers of these exceptional examples were always, or even often, able to combine dramatic expression with symmetrical versification. Side by side with Dalla sua pace we have Il mio tesoro and Non mi dir, in which exquisitely expressive opening phrases lead to decorative passages which are as grotesque from the dramatic point of view as the music which Alberic sings when he is slipping and sneezing in the Rhine mud is from the decorative point of view. Further, there is to be considered the mass of shapeless "dry recitative" which separates these symmetrical numbers, and which might have been raised to considerable dramatic and musical importance had it been incorporated into a continuous musical fabric by thematic treatment. Finally, Mozart's most dramatic finales and concerted numbers are more or less in sonata form, like symphonic movements, and must therefore be classed as musical prose. And sonata form dictates repetitions and recapitulations from which the perfectly unconventional form adopted by Wagner is free. On the whole, there is more scope for both repetition and convention in the old form than in the new; and the poorer a composer's musical gift is, the surer he is to resort to the eighteenth century patterns to eke out his invention.

THE NINETEENTH CENTURY

When Wagner was born in 1813, music had newly become the most astonishing, the most fascinating, the most miraculous art in the world. Mozart's Don Giovanni had made all musical Europe conscious of the enchantments of the modern orchestra and of the perfect adaptability of music to the subtlest needs of the dramatist. Beethoven had shown how those inarticulate mood–poems which surge through men who have, like himself, no exceptional command of words, can be written down in music as symphonies. Not that

Mozart and Beethoven invented these applications of their art; but they were the first whose works made it clear that the dramatic and subjective powers of sound were enthralling enough to stand by themselves quite apart from the decorative musical structures of which they had hitherto been a mere feature. After the finales in Figaro and Don Giovanni, the possibility of the modern music drama lay bare. After the symphonies of Beethoven it was certain that the poetry that lies too deep for words does not lie too deep for music, and that the vicissitudes of the soul, from the roughest fun to the loftiest aspiration, can make symphonies without the aid of dance tunes. As much, perhaps, will be claimed for the preludes and fugues of Bach; but Bach's method was unattainable: his compositions were wonderful webs of exquisitely beautiful Gothic traceries in sound, quite beyond all ordinary human talent. Beethoven's far blunter craft was thoroughly popular and practicable: not to save his soul could he have drawn one long Gothic line in sound as Bach could, much less have woven several of them together with so apt a harmony that even when the composer is unmoved its progressions saturate themselves with the emotion which (as modern critics are a little apt to forget) springs as warmly from our delicately touched admiration as from our sympathies, and sometimes makes us give a composer credit for pathetic intentions which he does not entertain, just as a boy imagines a treasure of tenderness and noble wisdom in the beauty of a woman. Besides, Bach set comic dialogue to music exactly as he set the recitatives of the Passion, there being for him, apparently, only one recitative possible, and that the musically best. He reserved the expression of his merry mood for the regular set numbers in which he could make one of his wonderful contrapuntal traceries of pure ornament with the requisite gaiety of line and movement. Beethoven bowed to no ideal of beauty: he only sought the expression for his feeling. To him a joke was a joke; and if it sounded funny in music he was satisfied. Until the old habit of judging all music by its decorative symmetry had worn out, musicians were shocked by his symphonies, and, misunderstanding his integrity, openly questioned his sanity. But to those who were not looking for pretty new sound patterns, but were longing for the expression of their moods in music, he achieved revelation, because, being single in his aim to express his own moods, he anticipated with revolutionary courage and frankness all the moods of the rising generations of the nineteenth century.

The result was inevitable. In the nineteenth century it was no longer necessary to be a born pattern designer in sound to be a composer. One had but to be a dramatist or a poet completely susceptible to the dramatic and descriptive powers of sound. A race of literary and theatrical musicians appeared; and Meyerbeer, the first of them, made an extraordinary impression. The frankly delirious description of his Robert the Devil in Balzac's short story entitled Gambra, and Goethe's astonishingly mistaken notion that he could have composed music for Faust, show how completely the enchantments of the new dramatic music upset the judgment of artists of eminent discernment. Meyerbeer was, people said (old gentlemen still say so in Paris), the successor of Beethoven: he was, if a less perfect musician than Mozart, a profounder genius. Above all, he was original and daring. Wagner himself raved about the duet in the fourth act of Les Huguenots as wildly as anyone.

Yet all this effect of originality and profundity was produced by a quite limited talent for turning striking phrases, exploiting certain curious and rather catching rhythms and modulations, and devising suggestive or eccentric instrumentation. On its decorative side, it was the same phenomenon in music as the Baroque school in architecture: an energetic struggle to enliven organic decay by mechanical oddities and novelties. Meyerbeer was no symphonist. He could not apply the thematic system to his striking phrases, and so had to cobble them into metric patterns in the old style; and as he was no "absolute musician" either, he hardly got his metric patterns beyond mere quadrille tunes, which were either wholly undistinguished, or else made remarkable by certain brusqueries which, in the true rococo manner, owed their singularity to their senselessness. He could produce neither a thorough music drama nor a charming opera. But with all this, and worse, Meyerbeer had some genuine dramatic energy, and even passion; and sometimes rose to the occasion in a manner which, whilst the imagination of his contemporaries remained on fire with the novelties of dramatic music, led them to overrate him with an extravagance which provoked Wagner to conduct a long critical campaign against his leadership. Thirty years ago this campaign was mentably ascribed to the professional jealousy of a disappointed rival. Nowadays young people cannot understand how anyone could ever have taken Meyerbeer's influence seriously. Those who remember how his reputation stood half a century ago, and who realize what a nothoroughfare the path he opened proved to be, even to himself, know how inevitable and how impersonal Wagner's attack was.

Wagner was the literary musician par excellence. He could not, like Mozart and Beethoven, produce decorative tone structures independently of any dramatic or poetic subject matter, because, that craft being no longer necessary for his purpose, he did not cultivate it. As Shakespeare, compared with Tennyson, appears to have an exclusively dramatic talent, so exactly does Wagner compared with Mendelssohn. On the other hand, he had not to go to third rate literary hacks for "librettos" to set to music: he produced his own dramatic poems, thus giving dramatic integrity to opera, and making symphony articulate. A Beethoven symphony (except the articulate part of the ninth) expresses noble feeling, but not thought: it has moods, but no ideas. Wagner added thought and produced the music drama. Mozart's loftiest opera, his Ring, so to speak, The Magic Flute, has a libretto which, though none the worse for seeming, like The Rhine Gold, the merest Christmas tomfoolery to shallow spectators, is the product of a talent immeasurably inferior to Mozart's own. The libretto of Don Giovanni is coarse and trivial: its transfiguration by Mozart's music may be a marvel; but nobody will venture to contend that such transfigurations, however seductive, can be as satisfactory as tone poetry or drama in which the musician and the poet are at the same level. Here, then, we have the simple secret of Wagner's preemminence as a dramatic musician. He wrote the poems as well as composed the music of his "stage festival plays," as he called them.

Up to a certain point in his career Wagner paid the penalty of undertaking two arts instead of one. Mozart had his trade as a musician at his fingers' ends when he was twenty, because he had served an arduous apprenticeship to that trade and no other. Wagner was very far from having attained equal mastery at thirty–five: indeed he himself has told us that not until he had passed the age at which Mozart died did he compose with that complete spontaneity of musical expression which can only be attained by winning entire freedom from all preoccupation with the difficulties of technical processes. But when that time came, he was not only a consummate musician, like Mozart, but a dramatic poet and a critical and philosophical essayist, exercising a considerable influence on his century. The sign of this consummation was his ability at last to play with his art, and thus to add to his already famous achievements in sentimental drama that lighthearted art of comedy of which the greatest masters, like Moliere and Mozart, are so much rarer than the tragedians and sentimentalists. It was then that he composed the first two acts of Siegfried, and later on The Mastersingers, a professedly comedic work, and a quite Mozartian garden of melody, hardly credible as the work of the straining artifices of Tanehauser. Only, as no man ever learns to do one thing by doing something else, however closely allied the two things may be, Wagner still produced no music independently of his poems. The overture to The Mastersingers is delightful when you know what it is all about; but only those to whom it came as a concert piece without any such clue, and who judged its reckless counterpoint by the standard of Bach and of Mozart's Magic Flute overture, can realize how atrocious it used to sound to musicians of the old school. When I first heard it, with the clear march of the polyphony in Bach's B mmor Mass fresh in my memory, I confess I thought that the parts had got dislocated, and that some of the band were half a bar behind the others. Perhaps they were; but now that I am familiar with the work, and with Wagner's harmony, I can still quite understand certain passages producing that effect organ admirer of Bach even when performed with perfect accuracy.

THE MUSIC OF THE FUTURE

The success of Wagner has been so prodigious that to his dazzled disciples it seems that the age of what he called "absolute music must be at an end, and the musical future destined to be an exclusively Wagnerian one inaugurated at Bayreuth. All great geniuses produce this illusion. Wagner did not begin a movement: he consummated it. He was the summit of the nineteenth century school of dramatic music in the same sense as Mozart was the summit (the word is Gounod's) of the eighteenth century school. And those who attempt to carry on his Bayreuth tradition will assuredly share the fate of the forgotten purveyors of second–hand Mozart a hundred years ago. As to the expected supersession of absolute music, it is sufficient to point to the fact that Germany produced two absolute musicians of the first class during Wagner's lifetime: one, the greatly gifted Goetz, who died young; the other, Brahms, whose absolute musical endowment was as extraordinary as his thought was commonplace. Wagner had for him the contempt of the original thinker for the man of second–hand ideas, and of the strenuously dramatic musician for mere brute musical faculty; but though his contempt was perhaps deserved by the Triumphlieds, and Schicksalslieds, and Elegies and Requiems in which Brahms took his brains so seriously, nobody can listen to Brahms' natural utterance of the richest absolute music, especially in his chamber compositions, without rejoicing in his amazing gift. A reaction to absolute music, starting partly from Brahms, and partly from such revivals of medieval music as those of De Lange in Holland and Mr. Arnold Dolmetsch in England, is both likely and promising; whereas there is no more hope in attempts to out–Wagner Wagner in music drama than there was in the old attempts—or for the matter of that, the new ones—to make Handel the starting point of a great school of oratorio.

BAYREUTH

When the Bayreuth Festival Playhouse was at last completed, and opened in 1876 with the first performance of The Ring, European society was compelled to admit that Wagner was "a success." Royal personages, detesting his music, sat out the performances in the row of boxes set apart for princes. They all complimented him on the astonishing "push" with which, in the teeth of all obstacles, he had turned a fabulous and visionary project into a concrete commercial reality, patronized by the public at a pound a head. It is as well to know that these congratulations had no other effect upon Wagner than to open his eyes to the fact that the Bayreuth experiment, as an attempt to evade the ordinary social and commercial conditions of theatrical enterprise, was a failure. His own account of it contrasts the reality with his intentions in a vein which would be bitter if it were not so humorous. The precautions taken to keep the seats out of the hands of the frivolous public and in the hands of earnest disciples, banded together in little Wagner Societies throughout Europe, had ended in their forestalling by ticket speculators and their sale to just the sort of idle globe-trotting tourists against whom the temple was to have been strictly closed. The money, supposed to be contributed by the faithful, was begged by energetic subscription-hunting ladies from people who must have had the most grotesque misconceptions of the composer's aims— among others, the Khedive of Egypt and the Sultan of Turkey!

The only change that has occurred since then is that subscriptions are no longer needed; for the Festival Playhouse apparently pays its own way now, and is commercially on the same footing as any other theatre. The only qualification required from the visitor is money. A Londoner spends twenty pounds on a visit: a native Bayreuther spends one pound. In either case "the Folk," on whose behalf Wagner turned out in 1849, are effectually excluded; and the Festival Playhouse must therefore be classed as infinitely less Wagnerian in its character than Hampton Court Palace. Nobody knew this better than Wagner; and nothing can be further off the mark than to chatter about Bayreuth as if it had succeeded in escaping from the conditions of our modern civilization any more than the Grand Opera in Paris or London.

Within these conditions, however, it effected a new departure in that excellent German institution, the summer theatre. Unlike our opera houses, which are constructed so that the audience may present a splendid pageant to the delighted manager, it is designed to secure an uninterrupted view of the stage, and an undisturbed hearing of the music, to the audience. The dramatic purpose of the performances is taken with entire and elaborate seriousness as the sole purpose of them; and the management is jealous for the reputation of Wagner. The commercial success which has followed this policy shows that the public wants summer theatresof the highest class. There is no reason why the experiment should not be tried in England. If our enthusiasm for Handel can support Handel Festivals, laughably dull, stupid and anti–Handelian as these choral monstrosities are, as well as annual provincial festivals on the same model, there is no likelihood of a Wagner Festival failing. Suppose, for instance, a Wagner theatre were built at Hampton Court or on Richmond Hill, not to say Margate pier, so that we could have a delightful summer evening holiday, Bayreuth fashion, passing the hours between the acts in the park or ontheriver before sunset, is it seriously contended that there would be any lack of visitors? If a little of the money that is wasted on grand stands, Eiffel towers, and dismal Halls by the Sea, all as much tied to brief annual seasons as Bayreuth, were applied in this way, the profit would be far more certain and the social utility prodigiously greater. Any English enthusiasm for Bayreuth that does not take the form of clamor for a Festival Playhouse in England may be set aside as mere pilgrimage mania.

Those who go to Bayreuth never repent it, although the performances there are often far from delectable. The singing is sometimes tolerable, and some times abominable. Some of the singers are mere animated beer casks, too lazy and conceited to practise the self–control and physical training that is expected as a matter of course from an acrobat, a jockey or a pugilist. The women's dresses are prudish and absurd. It is true that Kundry no longer wears an early Victorian ball dress with "ruchings," and that Fresh has been provided with a quaintly modish copy of the flowered gown of Spring in Botticelli's famous picture; but the mailclad Brynhild still climbs the mountains with her legs carefully hidden in a long white skirt, and looks so exactly like Mrs. Leo Hunter as Minerva that it is quite impossible to feel a ray of illusion whilst looking at her. The ideal of womanly beauty aimed at reminds Englishmen of the barmaids of the seventies, when the craze for golden hair was at its worst. Further, whilst Wagner's stage directions are sometimes disregarded as unintelligently as at Covent Garden, an intolerably old–fashioned tradition of half rhetorical, half historical–pictorial attitude and gesture prevails. The most striking moments of the drama are conceived as tableaux vivants with posed models, instead of as passages of action, motion and life.

I need hardly add that the supernatural powers of control attributed by credulous pilgrims to Madame Wagner do not exist. Prima donnas and tenors are as unmanageable at Bayreuth as anywhere else. Casts are capriciously changed; stage business is insufficiently rehearsed; the public are compelled to listen to a Brynhild or Siegfried of fifty when they have carefully arranged to see one of twenty–five, much as in any ordinary opera house. Even the conductors upset the arrangements occasionally. On the other hand, if we leave the vagaries of the stars out of account, we may safely expect always that in thoroughness of preparation of the chief work of the season, in strenuous artistic pretentiousness, in pious conviction that the work is of such enormous importance as to be worth doing well at all costs, the Bayreuth performances will deserve their reputation. The band is placed out of sight of the audience, with the more formidable instruments beneath the stage, so that the singers have not to sing THROUGH the brass. The effect is quite perfect.

BAYREUTH IN ENGLAND

I purposely dwell on the faults of Bayreuth in order to show that there is no reason in the world why as good and better performances of The Ring should not be given in England. Wagner's scores are now before the world; and neither his widow nor his son can pretend to handle them with greater authority than any artist who feels the impulse to interpret them. Nobody will ever know what Wagner himself thought of the artists who established the Bayreuth tradition: he was obviously not in a position to criticize them. For instance, had Rubini survived to create Siegmund, it is quite certain that we should not have had from Wagner's pen so amusing and vivid a description as we have of his Ottavio in the old Paris days. Wagner was under great obligations to the heroes and heroines of 1876; and he naturally said nothing to disparage their triumphs; but there is no reason to believe that all or indeed any of them satisfied him as Schnorr of Carolsfeld satisfied him as Tristan, or Schroder Devrient as Fidelio. It is just as likely as not that the next Schnorr or Schroder may arise in England. If that should actually happen, neither of them will need any further authority than their own genius and Wagner's scores for their guidance. Certainly the less their spontaneous impulses are sophisticated by the very stagey traditions which Bayreuth is handing down from the age of Crummles, the better.

WAGNERIAN SINGERS

No nation need have much difficulty in producing a race of Wagnerian singers. With the single exception of Handel, no composer has written music so well calculated to make its singers vocal athletes as Wagner. Abominably as the Germans sing, it is astonishing how they thrive physically on his leading parts. His secret is the Handelian secret. Instead of specializing his vocal parts after the manner of Verdi and Gounod for high sopranos, screaming tenors, and high baritones with an effective compass of about a fifth at the extreme tiptop of their ranges, and for contraltos with chest registers forced all over their compass in the manner of music hall singers, he employs the entire range of the human voice freely, demanding from everybody very nearly two effective octaves, so that the voice is well exercised all over, and one part of it relieves the other healthily and continually. He uses extremely high notes very sparingly, and is especially considerate in the matter of instrumental accompaniment. Even when the singer appears to have all the thunders of the full orchestra raging against him, a glance at the score will show that he is well heard, not because of any exceptionally stentorian power in his voice, but because Wagner meant him to be heard and took the greatest care not to overwhelm him. Such brutal opacities of accompaniment as we find in Rossini's Stabat or Verdi's Trovatore, where the strings play a rum–tum accompaniment whilst the entire wind band blares away, fortissimo, in unison with the unfortunate singer, are never to be found in Wagner's work. Even in an ordinary opera house, with the orchestra ranged directly between the singers and the audience, his instrumentation is more transparent to the human voice than that of any other composer since Mozart. At the Bayreuth Buhnenfestspielhaus, with the brass under the stage, it is perfectly so.

On every point, then, a Wagner theatre and Wagner festivals are much more generally practicable than the older and more artificial forms of dramatic music. A presentable performance of The Ring is a big undertaking only in the sense in which the construction of a railway is a big undertaking: that is, it requires plenty of work and plenty of professional skill; but it does not, like the old operas and oratorios, require those extraordinary vocal gifts which only a few individuals scattered here and there throughout Europe are born with. Singers who could never execute the roulades of Semiramis, Assur, and Arsaces in Rossini's Semiramide, could sing the parts of Brynhild, Wotan and Erda without missing a note. Any Englishman can understand this if he considers for a moment the difference between a Cathedral service and an Italian opera at Covent Garden. The service is a much more serious matter than the opera. Yet provincial talent is sufficient for it, if the requisite industry and devotion are forthcoming. Let us admit that geniuses of European celebrity are indispensable at the Opera (though I know better, having seen lusty troopers and porters, without art or manners, accepted by fashion as principal tenors at that institution during the long interval between Mario and Jean de Reszke); but let us remember that Bayreuth has recruited its Parsifals from the peasantry, and that the artisans of a village in the Bavarian Alps are capable of a famous and elaborate Passion Play, and then consider whether England is so poor in talent that its amateurs must journey to the centre of Europe to witness a Wagner Festival.

The truth is, there is nothing wrong with England except the wealth which attracts teachers of singing to her shores in sufficient numbers to extinguish the voices of all natives who have any talent as singers. Our salvation must come from the class that is too poor to have lessons.

nted in the United States
)83LV00004B/1/A